China and ASEAN: Pivoting Trade and Shock Transmission

Mala Raghavan · Faisal Khan ·
Evelyn S. Devadason

China and ASEAN: Pivoting Trade and Shock Transmission

Springer

Mala Raghavan
Tasmanian School of Business
and Economics
University of Tasmania
Hobart, TAS, Australia

Faisal Khan
Tasmanian School of Business
and Economics
University of Tasmania
Hobart, TAS, Australia

Evelyn S. Devadason
Department of Economics
University of Malaya
Kuala Lumpur, Malaysia

ISBN 978-981-16-1617-4 ISBN 978-981-16-1618-1 (eBook)
https://doi.org/10.1007/978-981-16-1618-1

This Springer imprint is published by the registered company Springer Nature Singapore Pte Ltd.
The registered company address is: 152 Beach Road, #21-01/04 Gateway East, Singapore 189721, Singapore

Preface

There have been many examinations of China's rise and participation in the regional and global economy. The trade interactions between China and the Association of Southeast Asian Nations (ASEAN), though extensively explored, are less understood in the context of its influence over the region amidst the recent changing dynamics that follow from China's global engagement. This volume focuses on the specific theme of the transmission of economic (output) shocks *via* the trade channel to inform the contemporary debate on the vulnerability of ASEAN to such shocks by providing a better understanding of the potential interactions between economic growth, trade and economic resilience. In particular, the chapters that comprise this volume highlight the critical relationship between China and ASEAN associated with its trade interdependency.

China plays an important role in the regional production chains, thereby promoting more intermediate goods transaction than that of consumption goods. As the largest trade partner for the region, China has presented itself with opportunities for ASEAN in tapping its market, but also great challenges given its dominant position in the regional production chains. The fundamental question that has motivated this volume, therefore, is whether China's engagement with ASEAN comes at a cost for the latter following from the systemic risks tied to the China-centric production chains in the region. Since the China-ASEAN trade relationship is multidimensional, in that its trading situation varies across the individual ASEAN Member States (AMS), the focus of this volume is on China's merchandise trade with the ASEAN6, the five founding members of ASEAN (Malaysia, Singapore, Thailand, the Philippines and Indonesia) including Viet Nam.

It is an academic volume that provides a comprehensive and coherent study of the transmission of output shocks *via* the trade channel with updated data and information. The recency in the data is particularly important as it captures the changing nature of trade and bilateral relationships between China and the AMS when examining the magnitude of the output shocks of the former on the latter. The methodology, though developed in our previous publications, are used here again in a somewhat or greatly different context to model the transmission of output shocks through the composition of trade, which are trade in intermediate (including capital goods) goods and consumption (final) goods. The empirical work in Chap. 3 and Chap. 4 also illustrates the transmission impacts based on the origin of the shock (regional shocks from the AMS and extra-regional shocks from the six interconnected economies outside the region, China, Japan, South Korea, India, Australia, and New Zealand), and the direct and indirect mechanisms of the trade channel.

Each chapter in this volume is written in a way in which the arguments are self-contained. The one exception is that the methodology introduced in Chap. 3 is a building block for Chap. 4. Chapter 4 substantiates the analyses of Chap. 3 by focusing on economic disturbances from China that are transmitted to ASEAN through the complex food production chain. The focus on food (including beverages) is warranted since it is an essential goods sector that is garnering much attention in the media, and thereby raising fears of food insecurity (in the context of food availability) among net food importers in the region, especially due to the disruption of cross-border shipments from the COVID-19 pandemic. The other reasons for focusing specifically on food are first, food is a highly regulated sector, and second, food, in general has high trade elasticities. The whole volume therefore adds up to present the main mechanism of the trade channel for the transmission of output shocks to ASEAN, and the comparative influences of China vis-à-vis other major extra-regional economies in propagating those shocks on the region.

This volume also resolutely rises against stereotypes and clichés, making readers reconsider many oversimplified assumptions of the benefits of trade engagement where economies are interconnected through complex production chains. We hope that not only academics, particularly economists, but all those wishing to make sense of China's trade impact, expanding influence, and consequences of trade linkages for the transmission of output shocks by putting it in a regional perspective, will find reading this book worthwhile for its specific details.

Finally, I thank Sarah Nur Syaza Mohd Yunos, the research assistant, for her help in data collection. The research on which this volume is based was supported by the Research University (RU) Grant—Faculty Programme, University of Malaya (Grant No: GPF005P-2019).

Hobart, Australia — Mala Raghavan
Hobart, Australia — Faisal Khan
Kuala Lumpur, Malaysia — Evelyn S. Devadason

Contents

About the Authors

Dr. Mala Raghavan is Senior Lecturer in Macroeconomics at the Tasmanian School of Business and Economics, University of Tasmania. Prior to joining the University of Tasmania in July 2011, she held academic positions at Monash University and RMIT University. She has more than 25 years of teaching experience at undergraduate and postgraduate levels at various universities across two continents—Australia and Asia (Malaysia, Singapore, and Hong Kong). She is also a Research Associate with the Asia Institute of Tasmania and a Visiting Research Fellow to Bank Negara Malaysia. Her publications include top ranking journals, such as *Energy Economics, Economic Modelling, Applied Economics, Economic Record* and *Canadian Journal of Economics*. She is involved in several collaborative projects associated with her work on the macroeconomic effects of various international and domestic shocks on small open economies, with focus on Asia. Her research partners include Bank Negara Malaysia, University of Calgary, University of Manchester, University of Newcastle, Monash University, Australian National University, Indian Institute of Management and University of Malaya.

Dr. Faisal Khan is Lecturer in Finance and Accounting at the Tasmanian School of Business and Economics, University of Tasmania. He is also a member of Chartered Accountants Australia and New Zealand (CAANZ), and is a Certified Practicing Accountant (CPA). He has extensive experience in the finance industry and academia in both Australia and Pakistan. His teaching and research experience extend over eight years. His current research work focuses on the evolution of international trade and its implications on Asian economies. He has been involved in various research projects, covering foreign investments, the emergence of China and the transmission of trade shocks across Asia Pacific economies.

Dr. Evelyn S. Devadason is Professor of Economics at the Faculty of Economics and Administration, University of Malaya. Her experience in teaching and research spans 25 years. Her research focuses on international trade and regional integration. Her research work has seen print in international journals, such as the *World Development, China Review, India Review, Pacific Review, Journal of Contemporary Asia, Journal of Contemporary China, Journal of International Development,*

Emerging Markets Finance and Trade, Asian Economic Journal, Global Economic Review, Singapore Economic Review, Social Indicators Research, among others. She currently serves as Editor-in-Chief to the *Institutions and Economies* journal, and Associate Editor to the *International Journal of Social Economics*, and a member to the Editorial Board of the *Journal of Contemporary Asia.* She has been engaged in a number of international research projects, including the International Confederation of Free Trade Unions—Asian and Pacific Regional Organization (ICFTU-APRO), Asian Development Bank Institute, Asian Development Bank, World Bank, Economic Research Institute for ASEAN and East Asia—United Nations Conference on Trade and Development (ERIA-UNCTAD), Food Industry Asia, United Nations Environment Programme-Denmark Technical University (UNEP-DTU) and the European Union H2020 Research and Innovation Framework Programme on Competing Regional Integration in Southeast Asia.

Acronyms

2SLS	Two-Stage Least Squares
ACFTA	ASEAN-China Free Trade Area
AFC	Asian Financial Crisis
AMS	ASEAN Member States
ASEAN	Association of Southeast Asian Nations
ASEAN6	Malaysia, Singapore, Thailand, the Philippines, Indonesia, and Viet Nam
BEC	Broad Economic Categories
DVA	Domestic Value Added
DVX	Indirect Value Added
FDI	Foreign Direct Investment
FTA	Free Trade Area
FVA	Foreign Value Added
GDP	Gross Domestic Product
GFC	Global Financial Crisis
GVC	Global Value Chain
HHI	Herfindahl-Hirschman Index
HS	Harmonized System
IIT	Intra-Industry Trade
MFN	Most Favoured Nation
NTB	Non Tariff Barrier
NTM	Non Tariff Measure
OLS	Ordinary Least Squares
RCA	Revealed Comparative Advantage
RCEP	Regional Comprehensive Economic Partnership
RD	Regulatory Distance
ROW	Rest of the World
SITC	Standard International Trade Classification
SPS	Sanitary and Phytosanitary
TBT	Technical Barrier to Trade
VAR	Vector Autoregressive
WTO	World Trade Organization

List of Figures

List of Tables

Chapter 1
China in ASEAN

1.1 Introduction

Economic (output) shocks, that could be transmitted from one country to another, are becoming increasingly important. In search for understanding the sources for such international spillovers, the ongoing debate among economists is whether international trade contributes to business cycles synchronization, or whether the observed correlation is simply a by-product of some other causal mechanisms (Boehm et al. 2019; Imbs 2004), such as economic conditions in the home country. Despite the difficulties in entangling the competing explanations, recent evidence suggests that the trade channel plays an important role in the cross-country transmission of output shocks (Lee 2019; Karim and Stoyanov 2020). The output shocks in major trading partners that are transmitted through trade linkages are in fact found to lead to large swings in the overall economy (Lee 2019). One important explanation behind this effect is the vertical linkages in production (Di Giovanni and Levchenko 2010; Escaith et al. 2010; World Bank 2020), which has created newer and faster channels for the propagation of adverse external shocks.

In line with the above arguments, the spillovers through output shocks is expected to be even more relevant for a highly trade integrated region like the Association of Southeast Asian Nations (ASEAN), which is closely linked through production chains. Concomitant to the increase in trade linkages within the region, the interconnectedness between the individual ASEAN Member States (AMS) and countries outside the region have also risen via vertical relationships (Nicita et al. 2013). The high trade linkages in the region, featured by intermediate[1] goods trade or value-added trade, may potentially have different implications for the transmission of output shocks from outside the region (Foster-McGregor and Stehrer 2013; Johnson 2014; Koopman et al. 2014). Three events have further brought to the forefront the importance of interconnections within ASEAN and between ASEAN and countries outside the region in its aggregate economic performance. Namely, the experiences from the financial crises [the 1997–1998 Asian Financial Crisis (AFC) and the 2008–2009 Global Financial Crisis (GFC)], the US-China trade war and the COVID-19

M. Raghavan et al., *China and ASEAN: Pivoting Trade and Shock Transmission*,
https://doi.org/10.1007/978-981-16-1618-1_1

pandemic have clearly shown that the dependence on production chains has created strategic vulnerabilities to the region.

China's engagement with Southeast Asia facilitated much of this build-up of regional production chains.[2] In fact, by 2010, China had already positioned itself at the manufacturing center of Southeast Asia mainly for assembly by lower-skilled workers and exports of finished products (Nicita et al. 2013; De Grauwe and Zhang 2016). Thereon, China had become increasingly important for regional suppliers of intermediate products, where there is localization of assembly operations to China, and a delocalization of the supply of part and components to other countries in the region. That such production chains often implicate China, has also led to claims that many countries, not just the AMS, have become too dependent or rather overdependent on Chinese supplies (Evenett 2020). It therefore came as no surprise when China emerged as a large exporter of "shocks" in 2006, at par with Japan, while Malaysia and Thailand were found to be the largest importers of such shocks (cited from Escaith 2009).

Arguably, while the greater interconnectedness of the region with China has resulted in gains in trade for ASEAN through the international division of labour and vertical specialization, the trade linkages fostered through production chains may also come with macroeconomic challenges for the region. Apart from that, the focus of this study on output transmissions in the China-AMS connections is also relevant as they involve large-small country pairs in which the large country, China, is an important trading partner to the AMS. While the large-small country case is recommended for addressing the identification problem mentioned above, which is however not relevant for this study since we are not comparing different shocks, the shock in the China (the large country) case appears identified because one has little reason to believe that such a shock represents responses to the small country's (individual AMS) own economic conditions (Schmitt-Grohe 1998).

The discussion on the transmission of output shocks raises a range of important questions for the ASEAN region. With a focus on the transmission of China's fluctuations to the AMS, this volume addresses those questions: How does ASEAN react to output shocks? What are the main trade channels behind the transmission of China's output shocks to ASEAN? How has China's growing engagement with ASEAN altered the transmission of output shocks to the region? How does China's role in the transmission of output shocks differ from shocks originating in other extra-regional trade partners of ASEAN? How does the trade channel further our understanding of what shapes the co-movement between China and the region, and China's influence as an exporter of shocks to the region?

The empirical work in this volume only considers the transmission of output shocks via the trade channel given the relevance of trade integration to the ASEAN region. The remainder of this chapter is structured as follows. The next section discusses the implications of the different mechanisms through the trade channel when examining cross-country transmission of macroeconomic (output) shocks. Section three provides an outline of the various chapters in this volume.

1.2 Transmission of Output Shocks: The Trade Channel

Several financial and non-financial or real (such as trade and investment) transmission mechanisms of output shocks have been proposed in the literature. Among those channels, a role has been attributed to the emergence of production chains, and to the different effects of the demand shock entailed by vertical linkages on trade and gross domestic product (GDP). Production chains serve both as transmission and amplification channels within the trade channel, and therefore have profound implications for understanding the transmission of output shocks across borders.

First, production chains render economies to be more susceptible to the transmission of output shocks through demand and supply, which can be amplified as they pass through the production chains to: (i) domestic industries (downstream/upstream linkages); or (ii) trade (export and import) linkages to other participating countries. In the case of the former, the story of production chains has been examined as a microeconomic shock (affecting only a firm or technology along the chains) from a localized disturbance (Carvalho 2014) in propagating impacts to the aggregate economy. In the case of trade, an external output shock from the trading partner through a supply shock that affects its industry supplying intermediate products ("compositional effect") would affect the downstream industries in the importing countries, as they are dependent on inputs from the country hit by the output shock. As for an external output shock in the partner country, from the demand side, amplification up the supply chain could further occur due to a "bullwhip" effect"[4] (Escaith et al. 2010; Altomonte et al. 2012), which then induces firms in the importing country to adjust their inventories to new expected levels of demand along the production chain (ECB 2016). Here again, the macroeconomic effect on inventories is amplified on the microeconomic side. This follows when output shocks from a particular source (for example, China) may be passed upstream through the production chain to input suppliers in other countries.

Second, production chains change the way economic shocks are transmitted to the region, depending on the role of the trading partner in the regional production chain. In short, they are transmitted via different trade channels, direct or indirect. As there could be several trade links for the transmission of the output shocks, the direct and indirect effects of those trade links are subject to various interpretations. For the empirical work in this volume, the direct and indirect effects are interpreted as follow. Direct effects refer to the influence of one country's output growth on that of another, through the bilateral trade connections between them. The indirect effects capture the impact of one country on another via its influence on the output growth of its trading partners—through supply chains and third markets. Indirect effects mean that shocks in one economy can affect other economies and regions despite weak direct trade linkages (Dungey et al. 2018). The indirect transmission of output shocks could be more complex than the direct transmission channel, especially for the outsiders, if they are highly connected with the regional production chains.

When examining the trade linkages perspective of cross-country macroeconomic shocks, the composition of trade flows becomes even more important since they mirror different trade elasticities (Bems et al. 2010; Escaith et al. 2010; Gangnes et al. 2012), depending on the sectoral composition and the degree of substitutability of the products being traded[5] (Burstein et al. 2008). These characteristics, including the length of the production chain, have implications for the intensity of the external shock.

There are reasons to believe that ASEAN may be relatively strongly affected more by component trade (trade in intermediate goods and capital goods) relative to final goods trade (trade in consumption goods), and more from demand developments in China relative to other major economies given China's central and dominant position in the regional production chains. Recognizing those expectations and that production chains have expanded asymmetrically across the region (Gangnes et al. 2012), this volume examines the cross-country linkages via the transmission effects on a select group of countries, the ASEAN6[6] (the five founding members of ASEAN, which are Malaysia, Singapore, Thailand, Philippines and Indonesia, and including Viet Nam) as a group (and the bilateral effects on the individual AMS). Viet Nam is included in the empirical analyses as it has emerged as an active player in the regional production chain (Obashi and Kimura 2016). The study only considers one source of shock, output shock, emanating from within ASEAN, China and other major economies outside the region (Japan, South Korea, India, Australia and New Zealand for purposes of comparison with China) (See Table A.1 for the sample of countries).

Thereafter, the transmission effects are considered through compositional effects on trade flows, based on two broad categories of products, intermediate and capital goods[7] (hereafter intermediate goods) and consumption goods (see Table A.2). This distinction between intermediate goods and final goods,[8] as explained above, matters as they account for the strength of the trade transmission channel, which then governs the strength of the demand spillovers from the economic shocks. This volume adopts the widely used reduced form empirical methodology to analyze the transmission mechanism, which is the vector autoregression (VAR) model. The VAR, the details of which are explained in Chap. 3, is used because it provides an appropriate framework in which to examine the transmission of output shocks. From the output shock, the response of the system to shocks by analyzing impulse responses (the propagation mechanism of the shocks), as well as output multiplier effects are then described. The data consist of quarterly observations from 1995 to 2018.

To compare the way in which the region and the individual AMS respond to output shocks from China, the same empirical framework is used for examining shocks from the other non-ASEAN members of the Regional Comprehensive Economic Partnership (RCEP)[9] Agreement. This permits an assessment of whether the response to output shocks in China is any different than in the other non-ASEAN RCEP members. The benchmark model constructed in Chap. 3 i s also used to explain the transmission of shocks through the food trade channel in Chap. 4. In a nutshell, the transmission of output shocks in both chapters considers the following trade channels: the origin of the shock (direct and indirect); the composition of trade flows (intermediate goods and consumption goods); and dynamic shifts in trade linkages.

The shifts in trade linkages estimated using time-varying export weights are important to identify changes in the patterns of transmission of idiosyncratic output shocks to aggregate fluctuations in output in the country of origin, China. This is because there could be some changes involving China's trade engagement with ASEAN as the structure of production chains is not static as explained hereon. First is China's own shifting role in the regional production chains, especially with the growing evidence of a reconfiguration of supply chains that has already begun in the pre-pandemic due to shifts in the Chinese public or rebalancing policy that encourages sourcing locally. The decline in foreign value-added (FVA) content[10] in China's gross exports from 17.91% to 11.12% between 2011 and 2018 (calculated from UNCTAD-Eora Global Value Chain (GVC) database 2020) suggests some economic balancing towards domestic supply and consumption (see also World Bank 2020). Second, is China's own dynamic transition into technology-driven activities (Abraham and Zhang 2020), which in turn are highly integrated globally (McKinsey Global Institute 2019). From that context, the differences in weights also capture how China interacts with the configuration of global demand changes to drive differences in the response of trade across the AMS.

This volume therefore contributes to the extensive literature on the propagation of economic shocks to ASEAN through a comprehensive account of the different mechanisms of the trade channel to understand China's trade impact regionally. Previous related studies for the region do not make this complete assessment (Abeysinghe and Lu 2003; Lau 2008; Feldkircher and Korhonen 2014; Sato and Shrestha 2014; Dungey and Vehbi 2015; Sato et al. 2011; Yuning and Junyi 2016; Ong and Sato 2018).

1.3 Outline of Monograph

This monograph contains 5 chapters. This chapter elaborates on the motivation for this study and frames the direction of this volume. Chapter 2 analyzes the shifts in the dynamic trade relationship and interdependence between China and ASEAN to set the background of the study. It provides some stylized facts on China's trade flows with ASEAN from the perspectives of trade balances, trade shares, participation in GVCs, trade in intermediate goods, product composition and product concentration.

Chapter 3 develops a formal model to provide an empirical assessment of output shocks of China on ASEAN6 based on its overall trade interdependence and its linkages through trade in intermediate goods and consumption goods. A comparative perspective is taken in this chapter, that is, shocks emanating from China are distinguished from direct shocks of the ASEAN region and indirect shocks from the other non-ASEAN members of the RCEP to provide context on the extent of influence of China on ASEAN6 relative to the latter two groups.

Chapter 4 furthers the investigation on the implications of the transmission of output shocks in Chap. 3 by taking a sectoral perspective to provide a richer description of trade interdependencies, and comparative effects of China versus regional and extra regional shocks. The food sector is chosen since modern food production involves extensive supply chains and multiple inputs, resulting in increasing trade linkages. As in the case of Chaps. 3 and 4 examines the extent to which the regional economies are affected through food trade by output shocks emanating from China relative to the other extra-regional trading partners.

The final chapter, Chap. 5, concludes with key inferences from the assessments of both the extent of interdependencies and effects of output shocks in understanding the economic resilience of the ASEAN region based on the direct and indirect trade channels. It also provides some policy recommendations for managing trade vulnerabilities and in developing better capacity for evaluating policy tradeoffs.

References

Abeysinghe, T., & Lu, D. (2003). China as an economic powerhouse: Implications on its neighbors. *China Economic Review, 14*(2), 164–185.

Abraham, F., & Zhang, Z. (Eds.). (2020). *China's rise and internationalization – Regional and global challenges and impacts*. World Scientific Publishing Co. Pte. Ltd.: Singapore.

Altomonte, C., Di Mauro, F., Ottaviano, G., Rungi, A., & Vicard, V. (2012). Global value chains during the great collapse: A bullwhip effect? Working Paper Series No. 1412, European Central Bank: Frankfurt.

Bems, R., Johnson, R., & Yi, K. M. (2010). Demand spillovers and the collapse of trade in the global recession. *IMF Economic Review, 58,* 295–326.

Boehm, C. E., Flaaen, A., & Pandalai-Nayar, N. (2019). Input linkages and the transmission of shocks: Firm-level evidence from the 2011 Tōhoku earthquake. *Review of Economics and Statistics, 101*(1), 60–75.

Burstein, A., Kurz, C., & Tesar, L. (2008). Trade, production sharing, and the international transmission of business cycles. *Journal of Monetary Economics, 55,* 775–795.

Carvalho, V. M. (2014). From micro to macro via production networks. *Journal of Economic Perspectives, 4,* 23–48.

Di Giovanni, J., & Levchenko, A. (2010). Putting the parts together: Trade, vertical linkages, and business cycle comovement. *American Economic Journal: Macroeconomics, 1*(1), 95–124.

De Grauwe, P., & Zhang, Z. (2016). The rise of China and regional integration in East Asia. *Scottish Journal of Political Economy, 63*(1), 1–6.

Dungey, M., & Vehbi, T. (2015). The influences of international output shocks from the US and China on ASEAN economies. *Journal of Asian Economics, 39,* 59–71.

Dungey, M., Khan, F., & Raghavan, M. (2018). International trade and the transmission of shocks: The case of ASEAN-4 and NIE-4 economies. *Economic Modelling, 72,* 109–121.

ECB. (2016). Transmission of output shocks—The role of cross border production chains. ECB Economic Bulletin Issue 2/2016. Retrieved from https://www.ecb.europa.eu/pub/pdf/other/eb201602_article01.en.pdf.

Escaith, H. (2009). Trade collapse, trade relapse and global production networks: Supply chains in the Great Recession. MPRA Paper 18274, University Library of Munich: Germany.

Escaith, H., Lindenberg, N., & Miroudot, S. (2010). International supply chains and trade elasticity in times of global crisis. Staff Working Paper ERSD-2010-08, World Trade Organization: Geneva.

Evenett, S. J. (2020). Chinese whispers: COVID-19, global supply chains in essential goods, and public policy. *Journal of International Business Policy, 3,* 408–429.

Feldkircher, M., & Korhonen, I. (2014). The rise of China and its implications for the global economy: Evidence from a global vector autoregressive model. *Pacific Economic Review, 19*(1), 61–89.

Foster-McGregor, N., & Stehrer, R. (2013). Value added content of trade: A comprehensive approach. *Economics Letters, 120*(2), 354–357.

Gangnes, B., Ma, A. C., & Van Assche, A. (2012). Global value chains and transmission of business cycle shocks. ADB Economics Working Paper Series No. 329, Asian Development Bank (ADB): Manila.

Imbs, J. (2004). Trade, finance, specialization, and synchronization. *Review of Economics and Statistics, 86*(3), 723–734.

Johnson, R. C., & Noguera, G. (2012). Accounting for intermediates: Production sharing and trade in value-added. *Journal of International Economics, 86*(2), 224–236.

Johnson, R. C. (2014). Trade in intermediate inputs and business cycle comovement. *American Economic Journal: Macroeconomics, 6*(4), 39–83.

Karim, R., & Stoyanov, A. (2020). Output volatility, composition of trade, and transmission of economic shocks across countries. *Review of International Economics, 28*(3), 626–655.

Koopman, R., Wang, Z., & Wei, S. J. (2014). Tracing value-added and double counting in gross exports. *American Economic Review, 104*(2), 459–494.

Lau, E. K. P. L. (2008). Interdependence of income between China and ASEAN-5 countries. *Journal of Chinese Economic and Foreign Trade Studies, 1*(2), 148–161.

Lee, D. (2019). Transmission of domestic and external shocks through input-output network: Evidence from Korean industries. IMF Working Paper WP/19/117, International Monetary Fund: Washington DC.

McKinsey Global Institute. (2019). *China and the World: Inside the dynamics of a changing relationship.* Brussels: McKinsey Global Institute.

Nicita, A., Ognivtsev, V., & Shirotori, M. (2013). *Global supply chains: Trade and economic policies for developing countries.* United Nations Conference on Trade and Development (UNCTAD): Geneva.

Obashi, A., & Kimura, F. (2016). Deepening and widening of production networks in ASEAN. ERIA Discussion Paper No. 2016-09, Economic Research Institute for ASEAN and East Asia (ERIA): Jakarta.

Ong, S. L., & Sato, K. (2018). Regional or global shock? A global VAR analysis of Asian economic and financial integration. *North American Journal of Economics and Finance, 46,* 232–248.

Sato, K., Zhang, Z., & McAleer, M. (2011). Identifying shocks in regionally integrated Asian economies with structural VAR and block exogeneity. *Mathematics and Computers in Simulation, 81*(7), 1353–1364.

Sato, K., & Shrestha, N. (2014). Global and regional shock transmission—An Asian perspective. CESSA WP 2014-04, Centre for Economic and Social Studies in Asia (CESSA), Yokohama National University.

Schmitt-Grohe, S. (1998). The international transmission of economic fluctuations: Effects of U.S. business cycles on the Canadian economy. *Journal of International Economics, 44,* 257–287.

Yuning, G., & Junyi, Z. (2016). Emerging China and its interaction with ASEAN economies. In Y.-C. Kim (Ed.), *Chinese global production networks in ASEAN* (pp. 1–18). Switzerland: Springer.

World Bank. (2020). *Trading for development in the age of global value chains.* Washington DC: World Bank.

Online Database

UNCTAD-Eora Global Value Chain (GVC) database. (2020). Retrieved from https://worldmrio.com/unctadgvc/

Chapter 2
Interdependent Trade Relationship

2.1 Introduction

China has ascended to become the world's largest exporter in 2010 and the largest trading nation in goods in 2013, by increasing its volume of exports and upgrading its contents (Caporale et al. 2015). Recording a surplus of USD359.248 billion in global trade, total trade of China reached USD46.292 trillion in 2018. While the world's exposure to China in trade has increased, China's exposure to the world has fallen in relative terms due to the rebalancing of the Chinese economy to domestic consumption (McKinsey Global Institute 2019). Having said that, exposure to China varies significantly across geographies.

From a regional context, the bilateral trade volume between China and ASEAN surged, from USD8.907 billion in 1992 to USD589.748 billion in 2018, at an annual growth rate of 18.53%. Specifically, trade relations between the two increased with China's accession to the World Trade Organization (WTO) in 2001. China and ASEAN have thus become each other's most important trading partners. The rise in exports of China was supported largely by the growth of imports of intermediate inputs from the region, including ASEAN. China therefore ran deficits in trade with ASEAN until 2011 (see Fig. 2.1), supporting its growth as the region's major market "creator" (Zhao et al. 2008; Devadason 2010; Yang and Martinez-Zarzoso 2014; Yu et al. 2014). Since 2012, China's imports from the region slowed down tremendously and recorded an annual average of 5.63%, while its export growth was maintained at a healthy 10.84%. This accounted for the change in China's trade status with ASEAN, trade deficit to trade surplus.

The unbalanced trade of China with the ASEAN bloc is therefore no longer just a phenomenon of its trade interactions with advanced economies. Nevertheless, some AMS outperformed their peers in trade with China. The trade balances of Malaysia and Thailand remained in their favour vis-à-vis China, while China recorded consistent trade surpluses with Cambodia, Lao, Myanmar, and Viet Nam for the entire period of review.

M. Raghavan et al., *China and ASEAN: Pivoting Trade and Shock Transmission*,
https://doi.org/10.1007/978-981-16-1618-1_2

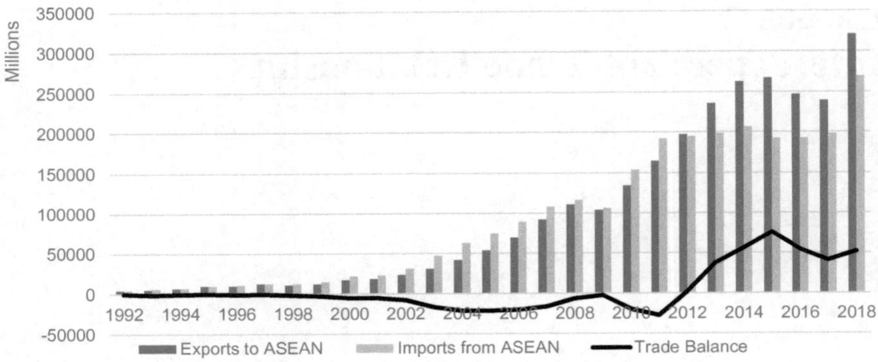

Fig. 2.1 China–ASEAN: Exports, imports and trade balance, 1992–2018 (USD million). *Source* UN Comtrade (2020)

This chapter provides an interpretation of the shifting position of China in the region, and how China and the regional concerns intersect and mutually affect their trade patterns and related policies.

2.2 China–ASEAN: From Grand Strategy to Regional Leader

China has indeed given priority to developing its collective relationship with ASEAN despite its complex links[11] with the individual AMS. Its regional economic cooperation evolved from the bilateral level to the regional level and beyond, ASEAN + 1, ASEAN + 3 (ASEAN + 3 Macroeconomic Research Office [AMRO]), ASEAN + 6 (RCEP), the East Asia Summit and the Belt and Road Initiative (BRI). China, therefore, is considered to have extended its influence on Southeast Asia through the afore-mentioned multi-layered structures.

From a trade perspective, the early 1990s witnessed many trade visits and diplomatic exchanges between China and the AMS. China began to view ASEAN as a potential trade ally and partner. Consequently, the period between 1990 and 1997 saw a dramatic increase in China–ASEAN trade. The turning point for this relationship was reached in the post AFC (1997–1998), with greater emphasis on trade. China, with its large home market base, projected itself as an "insulator" to external shocks (Ba 2003).

Subsequently, the ASEAN–China Free Trade Area (ACFTA)[12] was established in 2010,[13] following from the initial Framework Agreement signed in 2002 (Table 2.1). It is considered a fundamental step to strengthen trade activities between ASEAN and China (Zhao et al. 2008; Kim and Yen 2011; Wan-Ping and Jenn-Jaw 2014). Worth mentioning here is that the ACFTA, the largest free trade area (FTA) in the world in terms of population and the third largest in terms of GDP, is also recognized

Table 2.1 Progressive developments in China–ASEAN trade cooperation

Date	Description
China–ASEAN	
Nov-02	ASEAN and China signed the framework agreement on comprehensive economic cooperation (came into force on 1 July 2003)
2004	Launching of the Early Harvest Programme (EHP)—fast track trade liberalisation of agricultural products
Nov-04	Agreement on trade in goods (TIG) was signed (came into force on 20 July 2005)
Jan-07	Agreement on trade in services was signed (came into force in July 2007)
Jan-10	ACFTA was fully completed
Nov-15	Both parties signed the protocol to amend the framework agreement on comprehensive economic cooperation and certain agreements
Oct-19	ASEAN–China FTA upgrading protocol took full effect
China–Malaysia	
Apr-12	Registration of the Malaysian–China Business Council (MCBC)
Oct-13	Five-year programme for economic and trade cooperation was signed
China–Singapore	
Oct-08	China–Singapore FTA (CSFTA) was signed (came into force in 2009)
Nov-15	Launching of negotiations to upgrade the CSFTA; review to be completed by end of 2016
China–Thailand	
Oct-03	Sino–Thai FTA on trade in vegetables and fruits signed in June 2003, as part of the EHP, came into force
Oct-03	China–Thai FTA on trade in vegetables and fruits was signed on 18 June (came into force on 1 October 2003)

Source Compiled from media releases

as the most substantive agreement among all the ASEAN + 1 agreements. Through the 2004 "Early Harvest Provision," ASEAN gained an early opportunity to enter the China market under reduced (preferential) tariffs before the lower rates were extended to all WTO members. To allow the newer AMS to also take advantage of the early entrance into the China market before they themselves opened their own markets to Chinese competition as they had then still not joined the WTO, China extended its most favoured nation (MFN) status to the former. With the ACFTA, it appears that China became a priority market not just for the older AMS but also for the newer members of ASEAN.

In fact, China has remained ASEAN's top trading partner for 11 years. China has established trade relations with Singapore, Malaysia, Thailand, Indonesia, and Viet Nam. For China, the largest trading partners are the five founding members of ASEAN or ASEAN + 5 (Singapore, Malaysia, Thailand, the Philippines, and Indonesia) and Viet Nam. As shown in Table 2.2, the afore-mentioned six AMS or ASEAN + 6 accounted for 95.24% of China's total trade with ASEAN in 2018. A

Table 2.2 China—Export, import and total trade shares with AMS, 1992–2018 (%)

	Export share				Import share				Total trade share			
	1992	2000	2010	2018	1992	2000	2010	2018	1992	2000	2010	2018
Brunei	0.22	0.08	0.27	0.50	0.12	0.28	0.43	0.09	0.17	0.19	0.36	0.31
Cambodia	0.29	0.96	1.00	1.88	0.00	0.27	0.06	0.51	0.15	0.57	0.50	1.25
Indonesia	10.51	17.86	16.22	13.49	35.01	20.06	13.51	12.69	22.72	19.11	14.77	13.12
Lao PDR	0.62	0.20	0.36	0.45	0.08	0.03	0.39	0.75	0.35	0.10	0.38	0.59
Myanmar	5.76	2.91	2.58	3.30	2.96	0.57	0.63	1.75	4.37	1.59	1.54	2.59
Malaysia	14.37	15.01	17.61	14.30	18.68	24.97	32.75	23.53	16.52	20.63	25.70	18.51
Philippines	5.90	8.55	8.54	10.95	4.38	7.65	10.54	7.65	5.14	8.04	9.61	9.45
Singapore	45.10	33.81	24.04	15.54	27.81	23.04	16.06	12.50	36.49	27.75	19.78	14.15
Thailand	14.85	11.62	12.30	13.40	9.31	18.91	21.08	16.69	12.09	15.74	16.99	14.90
Viet Nam	2.38	9.01	17.08	26.20	1.64	4.23	4.54	23.82	2.01	6.32	10.38	25.11
ASEAN	100	100	100	100	100	100	100	100	100	100	100	100

Source Calculated from UN Comtrade (2020)

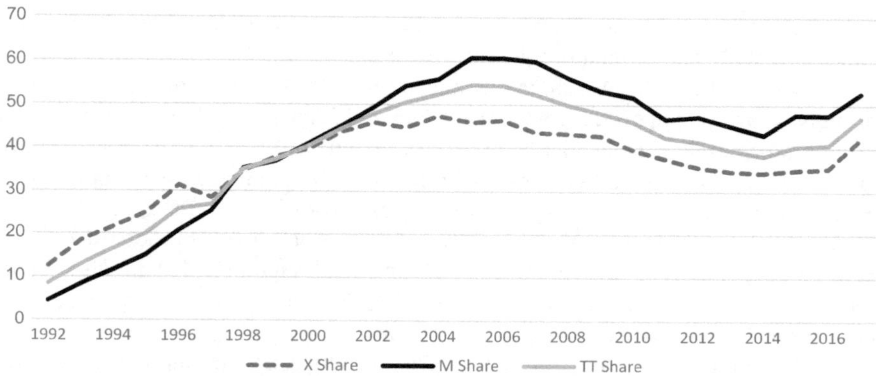

Fig. 2.2 China—Export, import and total trade shares of machinery/electrical products with ASEAN, 1992–2018 (%). *Note* Refers to HS 84–85 for machinery and electrical products. *Source* Calculated from UN Comtrade (2020)

major shift is that Viet Nam has overtaken Malaysia to become China's largest trade partner in ASEAN. This is due to the astonishing surge in China's exports to Viet Nam from USD106.233 million in 1992 to USD84.016 billion in 2018, having an annual growth of 32.91%. In 2018, Viet Nam commanded 26.2% of China's exports to ASEAN. Alternatively, Singapore's shares of China's exports and imports had dropped substantially.

China has indeed bolstered its trade leadership credentials with its commitments to market access through the concessions made in the ACFTA and the 2019 upgraded FTA protocol, and its role in the regional production chain (production networks) cooperation. Regional production chains form the backbone of China's trade with ASEAN, and the major source of that trade is machinery/electrical [(Harmonized System (HS) 84 and 85]. That category constituted 46.99% of China's total trade share with ASEAN in 2018, having increased from 8.53% in 1992 (see Fig. 2.2). Notwithstanding that, the product shares (exports, imports, and total trade) of electrical/machinery in China's bilateral trade with ASEAN declined gradually since 2006. Commanding higher shares of machinery/electrical in bilateral imports relative to exports, it appears that ASEAN is an important import source for China in the regional supply chain, especially since 2000. Though China remains a net importer of these products, but by country, China is only a net importer of machinery/electrical from Malaysia, Thailand, and the Philippines. China maintained trade surpluses in machinery and electrical trade with the remaining AMS. In fact, in the case of the China–Malaysia partnership, there is already clear evidence of overtrading in this category (Devadason 2015).

Not all AMS are deeply integrated into the regional production chains. For example, Brunei is not part of it, while the China–Indonesia and China–Philippines (to a lesser extent) exchanges resemble manufactures-for-resources. Since the density of the regional production networks lies in electronics, the dramatic rise in the share of machinery/electrical products in China's bilateral trade with Viet Nam from 7.57%

to 45.4% between 1992 and 2018 can also be interpreted as Viet Nam's deepening connection with the regional production networks.

Apart from the ACFTA, China's connections with ASEAN are also facilitated through expansions in border trade (Wan-Ping and Jenn-Jaw 2014). Border trade is of importance in the China–Viet Nam relations (Zhu 2008), as Viet Nam is the only country in Southeast Asia that borders China on both land and at sea. Commercial exchanges are prominent among the Vietnamese Northern provinces and Chinese provinces of Guangxi and Yunnan (Ngoc 2013). Apart from border trade, sub-regional cooperation such as the Greater Mekong Subregion (GMS) are also found to be important for enhancing trade (Hao 2008; Devadason 2013), specifically for the cases of China–Viet Nam and China–Thailand.

Another important strategy for trade expansion between China and ASEAN is the networks developed through Chinese businessmen. In this respect, the ethnic Chinese businessmen in ASEAN (namely Malaysia and Singapore) with their cultural affinity with mainland China, exploited their 'ethnic' advantage and intensified their trade interactions with China through business or commercial networks. The Malaysian Chinese entrepreneurs, through the Malaysian–China Business Council (MCBC) (see Table 2.1), has played an important role in this regard.

Clearly, the China–ASEAN connections matured into interdependence after the ACFTA, backed by their engagement in regional production networks. Following which, triangular trade patterns were formed among China, ASEAN and third country markets [namely developed countries outside the region, such as the United States (US), the European Union (EU) and Japan] (Yang 2013). This saw an increase in intra-industry trade (IIT), where ASEAN exported raw materials and manufactured parts and components to China to be further processed and assembled before exporting to third markets (Devadason 2011; Das 2013). China continues to play a pivotal and constructive role (Huang et al. 2017; IMF 2019) in those trade patterns.

2.3 China: Recalibration of Its Regional Position

China–ASEAN relations have entered a new stage, with ASEAN emerging as China's largest trade partner in 2020 (January–June), accounting for 14.7% of China's total foreign trade. This was brought about by the shifting of the production chains, namely in semiconductors. Following from the US–China trade war, China has been increasing its imports of chips from Southeast Asia and relocating its production bases to the region to circumvent US tariffs on Chinese imports. ASEAN has remained of equal importance as an import source and export destination for China, as shown in Fig. 2.3. In 2019, the region constituted 14.4%, 13.6% and 14.1% of export, import and total trade shares of China respectively. Specifically, the intensity of China's integration with ASEAN has increased with Viet Nam, Cambodia, and Malaysia over the last decade (OECD 2018). Following which, trade intensity between China and ASEAN is larger than expected given their importance in world trade, with the trade intensity index rising from 1.49 in 1990 to 1.82 in 2019 (UNCTADstat 2020).

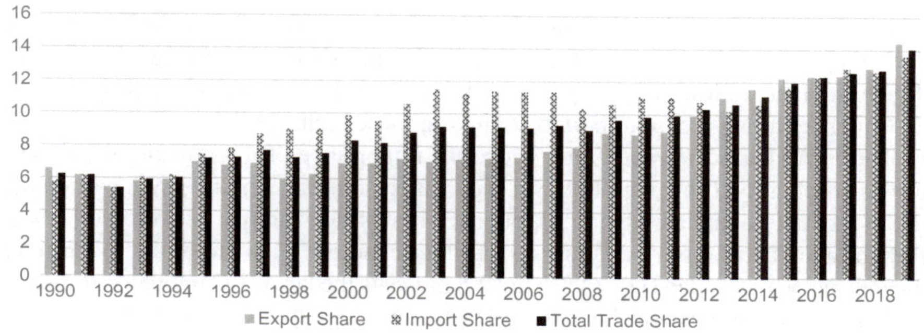

Fig. 2.3 China–ASEAN—Export share, import share and total trade share, 1990–2019 (%). *Notes* Export (import/trade) share is the percentage of exports (imports) going to a partner (from a partner/with a partner) to total exports (imports/trade) of China. A higher share indicates a higher degree of integration between China and ASEAN. *Source* ADB (2020)

China's integration with the region arguably intensified with the formation of regional specialization, characterized by intricate regional production sharing and trade in intra-regional networks. The latest GVC indicators provide a window into the participation of China and the AMS in GVCs. The shares of FVA in total exports of China and the individual AMS are presented in Fig. 2.4. Overall, the FVA shares in China are much lower than that for ASEAN, suggesting a shift towards domestic sourcing of intermediate inputs (see also OECD 2018). The shares of FVA in the total exports of ASEAN have reached a plateau for the period of review (35.84% in 1990 and 36.68% in 2018, after reaching its peak at 42.32% in 2008), while the

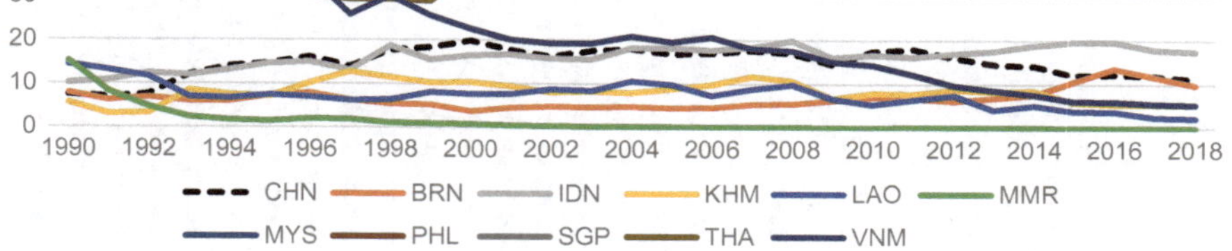

Fig. 2.4 China and ASEAN—Foreign value-added share in total exports, 1990–2018 (%). *Notes* CHN—China; BRN—Brunei; KHM—Cambodia; IDN—Indonesia; LAO—Lao, PDR; MMR—Myanmar; MYS—Malaysia; SGP—Singapore; THA—Thailand; PHL—Philippines; VNM—Viet Nam. The latest data available is 2018. *Source* Calculated from UNCTAD-Eora GVC Database (2020)

corresponding shares in China rose from 7.47% in 1990 to 17.91% in 2011 before declining to 11.12% in 2018. Across the AMS, the shares of FVA are highest for the Philippines, followed by Singapore, Malaysia, and Thailand, suggesting a higher dependence of exports on imported context in those countries.

The FVA shares, however, only gauge the importance of foreign suppliers backward participation (upstream links) in the value chain. Since many AMS participate in the production chain by being suppliers of inputs (forward participation or downstream links) used in third countries for further exports,[14] it is important to consider the indirect value-added (DVX). Figure 2.5 presents the key GVC indicators for each FVA, DVX and domestic value-added (DVA). There are two key observations. First, ASEAN is relatively more engaged with GVCs (FVA + DVX) than China. Table A.3 shows that the ASEAN6 (with the exception for Indonesia and to a lesser extent Viet Nam) are active participants in GVCs. Singapore is a forerunner in GVC. Viet Nam has become more involved in the GVCs, and the change in its participation has been mostly caused by the upstream part of the chain despite the sharp drop in its

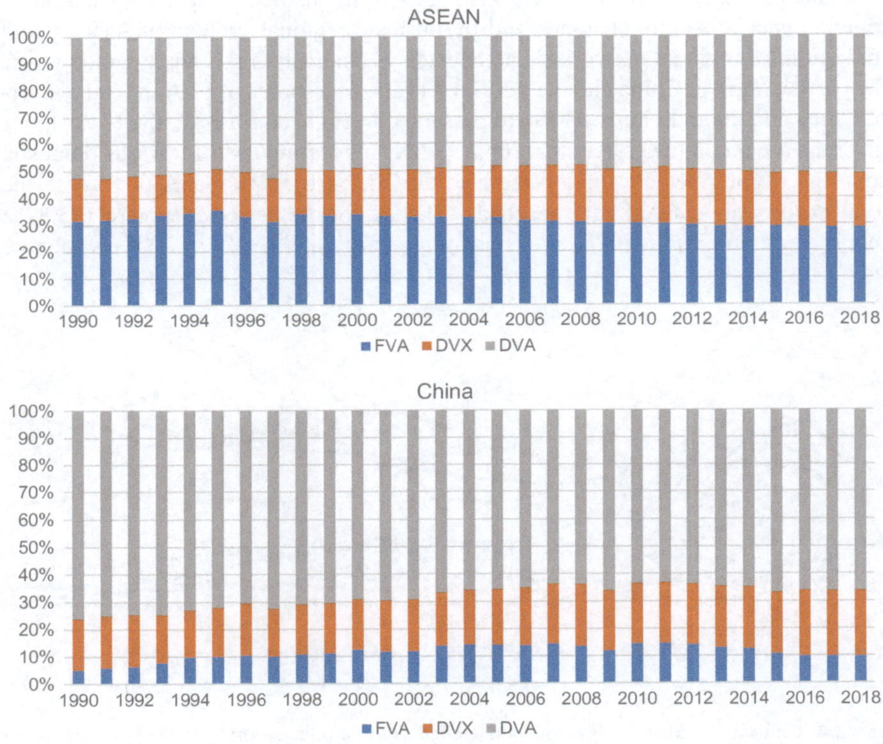

Fig. 2.5 China and ASEAN—Participation in global value chains, by FVA and DVX (%). *Notes* The latest data available is 2018. GVC = FVA + DVX, where GVC—global value chain; FVA—foreign value added; and DVX—indirect value added. *Source* Calculated from UNCTAD-Eora GVC Database (2020)

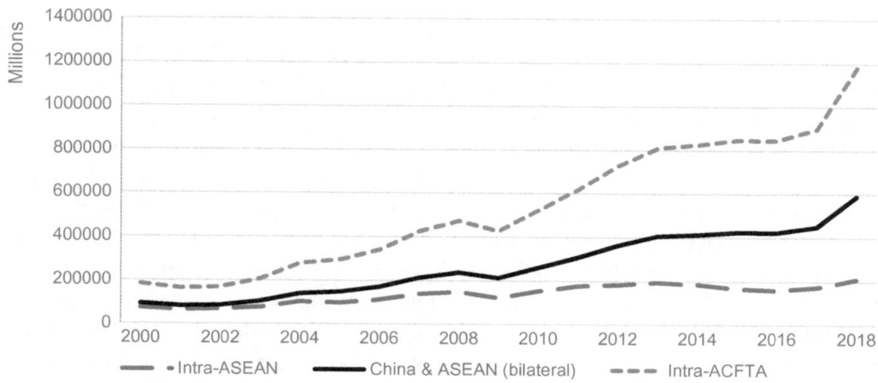

Fig. 2.6 China–ASEAN—Two-way export flows in intermediate goods, 2000–2019 (USD million). *Note* Based on the Broad Economic Categories (BEC; see Table A.2). It includes capital goods. *Source* UN Comtrade (2020)

share of FVA, as shown in Fig. 2.4. Second, ASEAN sources more inputs abroad, though they are now specializing more in the production of inputs at the beginning of the value chain (that is, the DVX is increasing over time; see also De Backer and Miroudot 2013). Conversely, China's participation in the GVC is higher as a supplier of inputs.

While the participation in GVCs are important for understanding the close trade connections of China and ASEAN with the rest of the world, the bilateral linkages also need to be identified to further support the arguments on the fragmentation of production from a regional perspective. China's bilateral engagement with ASEAN increased the total two-way export flows of intermediate goods[15] (see Table A.2 for the classification of goods) within the bloc, as shown in Fig. 2.6. Two-way bilateral China–ASEAN export flows of intermediate goods increased from 18.97% of total intra-ACFTA exports of intermediate goods in 2000 to 64.45% in 2018. China positioned itself as the manufacturing center for the region, mainly for assembly by lower-skilled workers and exports of finished products to countries outside the region. Thus, trade complementarity in certain product/technological categories (mainly in the electrical and machinery; see Fig. 2.2) accounted for much of the trade interdependence between China and ASEAN.

The trade complementarity story has changed somewhat. China no longer exhibits cost saving advantages like its ASEAN neighbour, Viet Nam, due to the rising cost of labour since 2004. The incremental labour cost subsequently caused a decline in the proportion of the labour intensive processing trade (with imported materials) since 2008. Comparative advantage based on cheap labour is no longer the driving force of China's engagement with the region. China has upgraded its industrial capacity from a mere assembler of imported inputs (Devadason 2009) to manufacturer along the middle and high-end of the global value chain (McKinsey Global Institute 2019). This is evidenced by an increase in its export quality since 2000 (Amighini 2005;

Fung et al. 2013; Ing et al. 2018; Yu 2020). Que et al. (2020) confirms that recent trends indicate a shift in the revealed comparative advantage (RCA) of China to hi-technology manufactured products, somewhat close to the levels of that of Singapore, Malaysia, Thailand, and the Philippines.

Table A.4 provides a comparative look of the RCA[16] for machinery and transport equipment [Standard International Trade Classification (SITC) 7, 3-digit level] for China vis-à-vis ASEAN between 1995 and 2019. China has increased its comparative advantage (RCA > 1), from 11 product categories in the SITC 7, 3-digit level, to 30 products between 1995 and 2019. Noticeably, China developed comparative advantages in office machines (SITC 75), telecommunications and sound recording equipment (SITC 76), and electric machinery (SITC 77) during the period under investigation. While China has been identified as having a comparative advantage in producing electrical equipment, China is found to be a net value-added importer[17] (Lu 2015; OECD 2018), which means that other economies add more value to its electrical equipment industry than China's own contribution of value added to the world electrical equipment industry.

The resulting effect of the industrial upgrading in China is a corresponding drop in imports of intermediates from the region (Lemoine and Unal-Kesenci 2002; Engardio 2007; ADB 2016). In that context, the possibility of China displacing ASEAN as an exporter in some product categories can also be inferred from the extent of product concentration.[18] Figure 2.7 shows that China has maintained consistently low levels of export concentration, comparable to that of Thailand, for the 1995–2019 period. For most countries, except for the Philippines, imports are marginally less concentrated than their corresponding exports. Unlike exports, the import concentration index of China has increased, albeit marginal, from 0.067 in 1995 to 0.173 in 2019.

Given the above illustrations, ASEAN is of no match for China, even in the low to mid-end products due to market power of the latter. Qin et al. (2013) assert that the trade relationships between China and ASEAN is one of asymmetric interdependence, and it is more radical at the country-level since it involves dynamic interactions between the AMS and China that can be both competitive and complementary (Chia and Sussangkarn 2006). More recently, Que et al. (2020) argue otherwise, claiming a shift in the China–ASEAN trade relationship; unidirectional ASEAN's dependence on China, rather than vice versa. The greater trade dependence on China somewhat reflects great exposure of ASEAN to China's increasing importance as a supplier and market for the region.

2.4 China-Centered Regional Order: Implications for ASEAN

Since the turn of the 21st century, China has brought a big change in the structure of relationships and order in ASEAN. Those relationships continue to be reconstructed with production chain linkages, external shocks from outside the region, and with

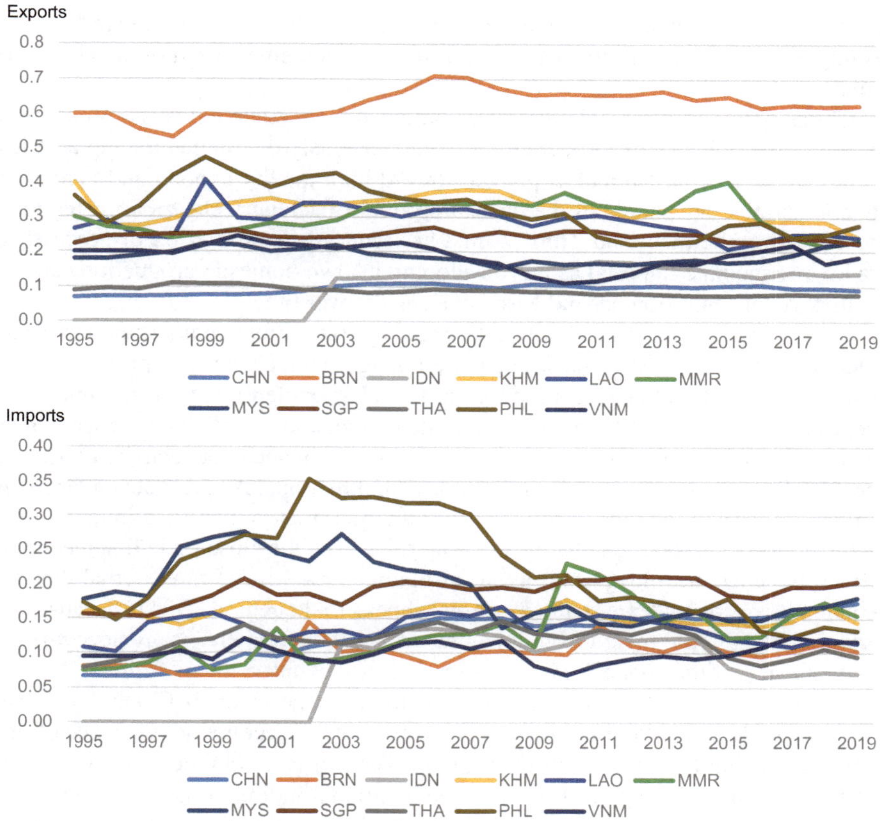

Fig. 2.7 China–ASEAN—Product concentration, 1995–2019. *Notes* CHN—China; BRN—Brunei; KHM—Cambodia; IDN—Indonesia; LAO—Lao, PDR; MMR—Myanmar; MYS—Malaysia; SGP—Singapore; THA—Thailand; PHL—Philippines; VNM—Viet Nam. The data for Indonesia is not available prior to 2003. *Source* UNCTADstat (2020)

the influence of extra-regional powers. Recent GVC indicators confirm the depth of the fragmentation of production. Close to half of the value of exports of AMS and China (to a lesser extent) is made up of products traded in the context of GVCs. Interestingly, ASEAN, on aggregate, participates in GVCs by not just sourcing inputs from abroad but also supplying inputs and increasing their "upstreamness."

The major changes in China's engagement with the world and the region, as revealed by the trade data, can influence the trade of AMS. The noteworthy trends from the bilateral trade data are summarized hereon. The trade status of China with ASEAN has shifted from a trade deficit to a trade surplus. Since China has intensified the flow of intermediate goods within ASEAN, China is not just important as a supplier, but also a market for the region. Sectors with a high level of integration, particularly those that are embedded in the production chains of machinery and electrical equipment are more exposed to China as both a supplier and market. For example, countries that produce inputs for further processing are exposed to Chinese imports.

China, however, is considered to have attained a complete industrial production system. First, China's exports are more homogeneously distributed among a series of products. Second, China has pivoted toward high-quality exports and increased its comparative advantage in the critical product (machinery/electrical) categories traded within the bloc; and Third, China has reduced its proportion of processing trade (intermediate imports) as it is developing its own domestic production chains; its import concentration has increased marginally over time.

From market "creator" and now a "priority" market, China remains an important trade partner for ASEAN. The strong trade linkages with China have produced both opportunities and challenges for the region. This chapter identifies two plausible challenges for the China–ASEAN dynamic trade partnership. The first challenge is that the asymmetric trade interdependent relationship established between the two since the ACFTA may slowly be shifting towards a unidirectional ASEAN dependence on China. The second challenge follows from the first, that is, the trade vulnerability of the region to production chain risks. The risks from the close trade linkages with China challenge the role of China as an "insulator" for ASEAN from external shocks, to China's role of an "exporter" of external shocks to the region. This is because the vulnerabilities in the region from manufacturing production chains are accentuated with so many of the connections going through one country, that is China.

The reality is production chains will continue to go through China and cross multiple borders and therefore it is timely to estimate the economic resilience of the region following from trade shocks in China. The degree of indirect dependence on China through the triangular trade and the additional indirect linkages established through the regional production chains with third party countries outside the region undeniably varies between the AMS. This warrants a country-level analysis of trade interactions between China and the individual AMS to provide meaningful insights into those partnerships.

References

Amighini, A. (2005). China in the international fragmentation of production: Evidence from the ICT industry. *European Journal of Comparative Economics, 2*(2), 203–219.

ADB. (2016). *Asian development outlook 2016: Asia's potential growth.* Manila: Asian Development Bank.

Ba, A. D. (2003). China and ASEAN: Renavigating relations for a 21-st century Asia. *Asian Survey, 43*(4), 622–647.

De Backer, K., & Miroudot, S. (2013). Mapping global value chains. OECD Trade Policy Papers, No. 159, OECD Publishing: Paris.

Caporale, G. M., Sova, A., & Sova, R. (2015). Trade flows and trade specialization: The case of China. *China Economic Review, 34,* 261–273.

Chia, S. Y., & Sussangkarn, C. (2006). The economic rise of China: Challenges and opportunities for ASEAN. *Asian Economic Policy Review, 1,* 102–128.

Das, D. K. (2013). China and the Asian economies: Mutual acceptance, economic interaction and interactive dynamics. *Journal of Contemporary China, 22*(84), 1089–1105.

Devadason, E. (2009). Malaysia–China network trade: A note on product upgrading. *Journal of Contemporary Asia, 39*(1), 36–49.

Devadason, E. S. (2010). ASEAN–China trade flows: Moving forward with ACFTA. *Journal of Contemporary China, 19*(66), 653–674.

Devadason, E. S. (2011). Reorganization of intra-ASEAN-5 trade flows: The 'China factor.' *Asian Economic Journal, 25*(2), 129–149.

Devadason, E. S. (2013). Whither sub-regional cooperation? The CLMV perspective. *Institutions and Economies, 5*(2), 1–36.

Devadason, E. S. (2015). Framing China–Malaysia trade relations beyond ASEAN: Factoring the regional comprehensive economic partnership. *Journal of Developing Areas, 49*(2), 39–56.

Engardio, P. (Ed.). (2007). *CHINDIA: How China and India are revolutionizing global business.* New York: McGraw-Hill.

Fung, K. C., Hwang, H.-C., Ng, F., & Seade, J. (2013). Production networks in China and India: A comparative analysis. *Economic Change & Restructuring, 46,* 45–69.

Hao, H. (2008). China's trade and economic relations with CLMV. In C. Sotharith (Ed.), *Development strategy for CLMV in the age of economic integration* (pp. 171–208). ERIA Research Project Report 2007-4-6. Chiba: IDE-JETRO.

Huang, Y., Salike, N., & Zhong, F. (2017). Policy effect on structural change: A case of Chinese intermediate goods trade. *China Economic Review, 44,* 30–47.

Ing, L. Y., Yu, M., & Zhang, R. (2018). The evolution of export quality: China and Indonesia. In L. Y. Ing & M. Yu (Eds.), *World trade evolution* (pp. 261–302). Abingdon, New York: Routledge.

IMF. (2019). *World economic outlook—Growth slowdown, precarious recovery.* Washington, DC: International Monetary Fund.

Kim, W. W. C., & Yen, M. Z. (2011). Economic relations between China and ASEAN, 1970–2010. *Chinese Management Studies, 5*(1), 20–34.

Lemoine, F., & Unal-Kesenci, D. (2002). China in the international segmentation of production processes. CEPII Working Paper No. 2002–02. Centre d'Études Prospectives et d'Informations Internationales: Paris.

Lu, Y. (2015). China's electrical equipment manufacturing in the global value Chain: A GVC income analysis based on world input-output database (WIOD). CAMA Working Paper No. 26/2015. Canberra: Centre for Applied Macroeconomic Analysis, Australian National University.

McKinsey Global Institute. (2019). *China and the world: Inside the dynamics of a changing relationship.* Brussels: McKinsey Global Institute.

Ngoc, N. T. B. (2013). Viet Nam–China economic relations and recommendations for ASEAN–China cooperation. In K. Young-Chan (Ed.), *China's policymaking for regional economic cooperation* (pp. 189–212). United Kingdom: Palgrave Macmillan.

OECD. (2018). Trade in value-added: China. Retrieved from https://www.oecd.org/industry/ind/TIVA-2018-China.pdf

Qin, F., Xu, T., & Zhang, Z. (2013). Economic cooperation and interdependence between China and ASEAN: Two to tango? In K. Young-Chan (Ed.), *China's policymaking for regional economic cooperation* (pp. 255–288). United Kingdom: Palgrave Macmillan.

Que, C., Zhang, F., Zhang, J., & Zhang, Z. (2020). Trade interdependence and comparative advantage between China and countries along the Belt and Road. In F. Abraham & Z. Zhang (Eds.), *China's rise and internationalization—Regional and global challenges and impacts* (pp. 37–66). Singapore: World Scientific Publishing Co., Pte. Ltd.

Wan-Ping, T., & Jenn-Jaw, S. (2014). Trade relations between China and Southeast Asia. *The Chinese Economy, 47*(3), 23–39.

Yang, J. (2013). *China's policymaking for regional economic cooperation.* Hampshire: Palgrave MacMillan.

Yang, S., & Martinez-Zarzoso, I. (2014). A panel data analysis of trade creation and trade diversion effects: The case of ASEAN–China free trade area. *China Economic Review, 29,* 138–151.

Yu, S., Hsiao, C. T., & Xinpeng, X. (2014). The impact of the ACFTA on ASEAN–PRC trade: Estimates based on an extended gravity model for component trade. *Applied Economics, 46*(19), 2251–2263.

Yu, M. (2020). *China–US trade war and trade talk*. Singapore: Springer Nature Singapore Pte Ltd.

Zhao, L., Malouche, M., & Newfarmer, R. (2008). China's emerging regional trade policy. *Journal of Chinese Economic and Foreign Trade Studies, 1*(1), 21–35.

Zhu, Z. (2008). China's opening-up strategy and its economic relations with ASEAN countries—A case study of Yunnan province. Visiting Research Fellow Monograph Series No. 435. Institute of Developing Economies, JETRO: Japan.

Online Databases

Asian Development Bank (ADB). (2020). Asia Regional Integration Center—Integration Indicators. Retrieved from https://aric.adb.org/database/integration

UN Comtrade. (2020). Retrieved from https://comtrade.un.org/data/

UNCTAD-Eora Global Value Chain (GVC) Database. (2020). Retrieved from https://worldmrio.com/unctadgvc/

UNCTADstat. (2020). Retrieved from https://unctadstat.unctad.org/wds/ReportFolders/reportFolders.aspx?sCS_ChosenLang=en

Chapter 3
Trade Shocks and Resiliency

3.1 Introduction

The ASEAN economies have undergone profound changes over the past two decades because of globalization and the emergence of China, India, and other economies as global economic players. As a result, the transmission mechanisms of the international business cycle to ASEAN have changed. Recognizably, China has penetrated the ASEAN merchandise market more efficiently than the other way around post ACFTA, resulting in China enjoying trade surpluses (Chiang 2019) with the region. China's centrality in ASEAN began with the rise of regional production chains, whereby manufactured intermediates from ASEAN were exported for assembly in China. Despite some changes in the relations within the production chains due to industrial upgrading/adjustment in China and some AMS, China remains its dominant position in 'Factory Asia.'

Evidently, China's extensive linkages with ASEAN has resulted in spill-over effects that are detrimental to the latter. The increasing trade linkages led to co-movements and increased volatility as they induced large demand-side effects. For example, the current US-China trade war caused a realignment of global supply chains in the ASEAN region, namely in Malaysia, Thailand, and Viet Nam (Tobin and Power 2019). The role of China on the propagation of trade shocks to ASEAN may therefore prove to be somewhat different given its varying trade dynamics with the region, as discussed in Chap. 2.

Despite the empirical research devoted to evaluating the role of trade in the international propagation mechanism, no consensus has been reached to date on the importance of trade links in transmitting economic shocks (Dungey et al. 2018). It is therefore imperative to examine this issue in the context of ASEAN, a highly integrated region that is wanting to work more closely with China to counter the pressure of protectionism and ensure continued growth (East Asia Pacific, 28 April 2018). Further, the expected enhancement of trade linkages of China with ASEAN under the RCEP structure, raises the importance of examining its role in transmitting trade shocks to the region, directly and indirectly through other countries in the region.

M. Raghavan et al., *China and ASEAN: Pivoting Trade and Shock Transmission*,
https://doi.org/10.1007/978-981-16-1618-1_3

Against the backdrop of asymmetric trade interdependencies in the China-ASEAN bilateral relations, this chapter captures the degree of exposure of the individual AMS (with a special focus on ASEAN6) to trade shocks[19] in China to better understand the effects of cross-country linkages. A valuable extension to previous related research, as deliberated in Chap. 1, is the use of trade measures beyond total export shares/concentration to export shares of intermediate goods, when capturing the direct and indirect trade linkages.

This chapter focuses on the emergence of China as a global force in the world economy and investigates how changes in trade patterns between China and the non-ASEAN RCEP members have affected the transmission of the international business cycle to ASEAN6. Specifically, we investigate empirically how shocks to output growth in China are transmitted to ASEAN6, conditional on alternative configurations of cross-country linkages in the world economy. We focus on China because its trade linkages with ASEAN6 have undergone major shifts over the period considered. We also focus on Japan and South Korea because these economies are important trading partners of ASEAN6. To complement this analysis, we also considered the impact of intra-ASEAN6 shocks as the analysis of these shocks helps shed light on the business cycle and interdependence of these economies. The rest of the chapter is organized as follows. Section 3.2 reviews the extant literature. Section 3.3 describes the data and changes in output growth and export-shares. Section 3.4 explains the methodology and estimation procedures. Section 3.5 presents the empirical results and Sect. 3.6 concludes.

3.2 Related Literature

Bilateral trade is an important source for inter-country business cycle linkages (Imbs 2004; Baxter and Kouparitsas 2005; Cheewatrakoolpong and Manprasert 2014). Increasing trade links may therefore lead to co-movements and increased volatility as they induce large demand-side (contraction, expansion, and substitution) effects. In the presence of production chains, like the case of China's engagement with ASEAN, the emphasis on common global (external) shocks is understandable, as the effects of the shocks can be transmitted indirectly through induced changes in domestic production and trade, and intermediate goods (Cheewatrakoolpong and Manprasert 2015; Sato and Shrestha 2014). Arguably, the transmission of shocks in the presence of production chains can magnify regional or global shocks.

The literature on the trade channel, more specifically as a transmission mechanism for propagating shocks across countries, however, remains at best mixed. Several studies find a moderate or weak role for trade interdependence in propagating economic shocks (Canova 1991; Canova and Dellas 1993; Masson 1999; Baig and Goldfajn 1999; Harrigan 2000; Blanchard et al. 2010 and Berkmen et al. 2012). Alternatively, studies by Dungey and Martin (1998), Ito and Hashimoto (2005) and Haidar (2012) identify that trade (both bilateral and competition via a third market) had some influences in explaining the propagation of instabilities and output shocks in the international markets.

Both theoretical and empirical evidence confirm the presence of various channels and greater integration may influence the relationship between country or region-specific economic shocks. Frankel and Rose (1998), Clark and Van Wincoop (2001) and Kose and Yi (2006) demonstrate that business cycles of economies with greater trade links are more correlated. Gruben et al. (2002) verify the proposition of a positive link between closer trade ties and synchrony of business cycles, while Calderon et al. (2007) found a substantial direct impact of trade on business cycle co-movements for emerging countries.

Economic shocks may spread internationally via income effects and product competitiveness. The demand contraction and income effects have sizeable influence on the spillover of uncertainties in export-dependent economies (Perry and Lederman 1998). Rose and Spiegel (2011) and da Costa Neto and Romeu (2011), on the other hand, dispute this view by demonstrating that destination export concentration is not significant in disseminating shocks. Further, Kurz and Senses (2016), Caselli et al. (2015), Cavallo and Frankel (2008) argue that trade openness reduces the exposure of economies to external shocks, while Edwards (2004) and Martin and Rey (2006) emphasize that developing economies with limited trade openness and increased financial integration are at higher risk from economic disruptions. However, Forbes (2004) points out that if the income effect amplifies with currency devaluation, it can lead to further reduction of real incomes. Currency devaluation leads to changes in international competitiveness as relative prices shift for trade partners, leading to not only direct but also indirect effects on both the traded and non-traded sectors via income effects, which then feedback to other trading partners, known as the third market effects.

Increasing trade links and intensity among various regions and economies may increase the business cycle synchronization and amplify the transmission of international economic shocks. Kali and Reyes (2010) and Kuroiwa and Kuwamori (2010) demonstrate that extensive trade links increase a country's exposure to international shocks, while Fidrmuc and Korhonen (2010) show that stronger trade links lead to a greater synchronization of recessionary shocks. Concentrated trade linkages can strengthen cross border inter-dependence by inducing large demand side effects. For instance, a positive output growth shock stimulates a rising external demand in one country and thus boosts the economy of its trading partners. Baxter and Kouparitsas (2005) assess a large sample of both developed and emerging economies and found trade intensity amplifies business-cycle correlations. Giovanni and Levchenko (2012) and Feldkircher (2014) conclude that trade openness substantially amplifies the transfer of instability rather than mitigating it, while Dungey et al. (2014) confirm the validity of the trade-channel for the propagation of shocks, concluding that the effect of a shock increases as economic linkages deepen amongst the regions and countries.

Another important channel for the integration of business cycles across countries is through IIT trade linkages. Imbs (2004), and Shin and Wang (2005) find that international business cycle transmits mainly via IIT links. Focusing on the Euro Area,

Zervoyianni and Anastasiou (2009) show that demand spillovers and IIT are dominant in the international propagation of shocks via trade, while Burstein et al. (2008) and Kappler (2011) contend that IIT helps to explain the variation of business cycle synchronization. Dées and Zorell (2012) disentangle the role of trade links through different sectoral specialization. Their findings confirm that when an economy is heavily export dependent on partner economies, which are affected by crises, the affected sectors arguably act as significant transmission channels. Pentecôte and Rondeau (2015) point out that a decline of output (industrial production) because of an output shock internationally is smaller in countries restraining trade than in those promoting transnational trade, consistent with the findings of Abeysinghe and Forbes (2005).

In this chapter we also analyze the different IIT linkages by focusing on two broad categories of goods, namely the intermediate goods and consumption goods. The transmission of shocks in output to other economies *via* trade linkages are assessed through these two trade channels. As in Abeysinghe and Forbes (2005), Hesse (2008), Sato and Shrestha (2012), Cheewatrakoolpong and Manprasert (2014), and Dungey et al. (2018), we proceed to analyze both direct and indirect transmission channels as both are found to be important in the literature. Tan et al. (2015) and Cheewatrakoolpong and Manprasert (2015) demonstrate that indirect trade connections with other economies are vital for understanding the transmission patterns as they occur via transnational trade-channels.

Unfortunately, the literature on trade interdependencies is often done in an off-model manner, casting doubts on the findings. A caveat on standard econometric models that seek to address this subject is that they still lack a coherent global dimension, which is essential for examining macroeconomic cross-country linkages. The methodological issues will be discussed in detail under Sect. 3.4.

3.3 Output Growth and Trade Patterns Among RCEP Members

This section details the data, namely the output and trade patterns between ASEAN6 and the rest of the RCEP members. It also provides a cursory look of the core data patterns related to GDP growth rates and export shares of two broad categories of goods—intermediate goods and consumption goods. The list of the 12 countries (ASEAN6 and non-ASEAN RCEP members) included in our analysis are provided in Table A.1.

3.3.1 Data Description

Quarterly GDP and bilateral export shares of two broad categories of goods—intermediate goods (including capital goods, as explained in Chap. 1) and consumption goods of ASEAN, China, and the rest of the RCEP economies are used respectively to measure output and export linkages between them. The data for the empirical analyses come from multiple sources.

Quarterly GDP data is extracted from the International Financial Statistics (IFS), Datastream and CEIC databases. Since the GDP series are largely measured in domestic currencies, the series is transformed and expressed in US (million) dollars, using official bilateral US exchange rates of the respective countries that are sourced from the CEIC and World Development Indicators (WDI) of the World Bank (2020). Output growth rates are measured as first differences of log real GDP, where the X-12 procedure is applied when seasonal adjustment is required. Descriptive statistics of the output growth series for the 12 countries can be found in Table A.5. As reported in Table A.6, the output growth series of all countries included in our sample are stationary.

The annual intermediate exports, capital exports and consumption exports data, reported in current US dollars, are sourced from the BEC of the UN Comtrade (2020) database. Based on the BEC, intermediate and capital goods are for industrial and primary sector purposes, while consumption goods are for household purposes (see Table A.2). We are considering these two broad categories of goods, to assess the transmission of China's output shocks on ASEAN6 based on its trade interdependence and its linkages through these two different trade channels. A comparative perspective is also taken with the ASEAN region and the non-ASEAN members of the RCEP (RCEP subgroup, excluding China—Japan, South Korea, Australia, New Zealand and India) to provide context on the extent of influence of China on ASEAN6 relative to the latter two groups.

The final database contains 12 GDP growth series and 144 export share series for intermediate and capital goods, and for consumption goods, respectively. This includes ASEAN6, the non-ASEAN RCEP members and the rest of the world (ROW). ROW is estimated as a control and contains all member countries of the world except for the 12 economies in our dataset. The sample period extends from the 1st quarter of 1995 to the 4th quarter of 2018.

3.3.2 Output Growth Patterns of ASEAN6

This section develops an assessment of the cross-country variation in bilateral output growth correlations of the ASEAN6 economies with China and other non-ASEAN members of RCEP. We focus on growth rates of GDP as our means of identifying common cycles in these economies as growth rates have the advantage of being a natural measure of how economies perform over the economic cycle.[20]

Table 3.1 presents pairwise correlations of quarterly GDP growth series between the RCEP members. We find that 50% of the values are statistically significant at the 5% level. The significant correlation coefficients among the ASEAN6 economies imply relatively close business cycle synchronization among the economies in the region. This is obvious between Malaysia with Singapore, Indonesia, and the Philippines, where the correlation is around 55%. A strong business cycle synchronization is also observed between the ASEAN6 members with South Korea and Japan. As stated by Otto et al. (2001), there could be two potential explanations for the correlation of output growth. First, a country or region-specific shock is transmitted through various economic interdependencies between these countries, partly due to less diversified production and specialisation effects. The second explanation is that there are common shocks affecting these economies, and countries with similar economic structure are likely to be highly correlated. For example, increasing trade links may lead to co-movements of the business cycle and output volatility as the trading economies are exposed to a common shock underlying the cyclic behaviour.

We examine the pattern of the bilateral correlations over time by plotting the correlations for the period 1995 to 2018. Figures 3.1 and 3.2 plot rough measures of business cycle synchronization; a 10-year rolling window correlation between ASEAN6 and China, and other RCEP members' GDP growth rates.

Figure 3.1 shows the bilateral output growth rate correlation of the ASEAN6 as a group with each of the other non-ASEAN RCEP members. Not surprisingly, Fig. 3.1 indicates, among the highly correlated economies, are pairs of ASEAN6 with the East Asian economies, namely China, Japan, and South Korea. Since 2000, the positive relationships between ASEAN6 with these economies have been growing, implying a rising business cycle synchronization between these economies. In 2010, following the GFC, the average rolling correlation between ASEAN6 and China stood at a level four times more than in 1999; increasing from 0.1 to 0.5. ASEAN6's average correlation with Japan and South Korea were strong in 1999, around 0.4 and 0.7 and in 2010, 0.7 and 0.5 respectively. The ASEAN6's strong and rising integration with East Asian partners could be through trade, and possibly through the initiatives for greater economic and political integration.

Figure 3.2 provides the bilateral output growth rate correlations of the individual ASEAN6 economies with China. Indonesia, Malaysia, Singapore, and Thailand display similar average rolling correlation patterns with China, and the relationships have been positive and rising. The negative correlations observed in the earlier part of the sample appear to be transitory. In the post AFC period, the economic growth patterns of the ASEAN6 seem to be tracking closely with that of China. After the GFC, the positive relationship is found to be still strong (except for Viet Nam and the Philippines). This observation however does not resonate with the findings of Yuning and Junyi (2016), as they claim that ASEAN has become less integrated with China in terms of output growth after the GFC.

It can be taken as evidence that the changes in the international economic environment have shifted the nature of the relationships between these economies. For example, if trade relationships were principally responsible for the correlation of GDP growth with China, then the changing pattern of correlations could reflect

Table 3.1 Correlation matrix, 1995Q1 to 2018Q4

	IDN	MYS	PHL	SGP	THA	VNM	CHN	JPN	KOR	AU	NZ	IND
IDN	1.000											
MYS	**0.568**	1.000										
PHL	**0.364**	**0.553**	1.000									
SGP	**0.264**	**0.549**	**0.386**	1.000								
THA	**0.386**	**0.376**	**0.277**	**0.310**	1.000							
VNM	0.174	**0.272**	**0.257**	0.124	0.167	1.000						
CHN	−0.055	0.195	0.112	**0.363**	**0.297**	0.146	1.000					
JPN	0.147	**0.425**	**0.421**	**0.402**	**0.374**	0.157	**0.306**	1.000				
KOR	**0.416**	**0.625**	**0.295**	**0.437**	**0.327**	0.137	0.106	**0.298**	1.000			
AU	−0.116	−0.015	−0.047	0.192	0.057	0.008	**0.241**	0.071	0.159	1.000		
NZ	**0.267**	**0.377**	**0.265**	**0.320**	**0.413**	0.191	0.118	0.168	**0.309**	**0.226**	1.000	
IND	0.035	0.008	0.023	0.015	−0.157	0.106	0.076	0.038	−0.138	0.031	−0.012	1.000

Notes The bold figures represent values that are statistically significant at the 5% level. See Table A.1 for country codes
Source Authors' own estimation

Fig. 3.1 Bilateral output growth correlations between ASEAN6 and non-ASEAN RCEP, 1995–2018. *Notes* This figure plots 10-year rolling window correlations of annual output growth rates from 1995Q1 to 2018Q4. *Source* Authors' own estimation

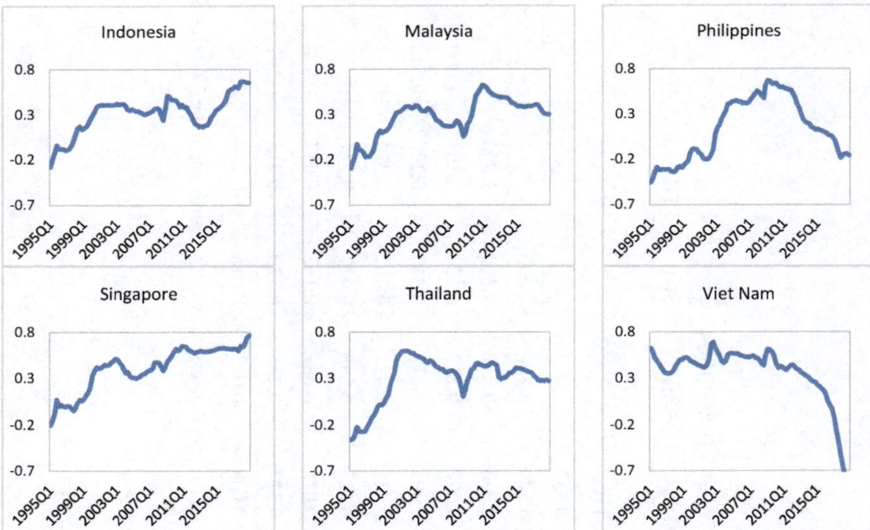

Fig. 3.2 Output co-movements between ASEAN6 with China, 1995–2018. *Notes* This figure plots 10-year rolling window correlations of annual output growth rates from 1995Q1 to 2018Q4. *Source* Authors' own estimation

changing patterns of trade. This is explored in the next section. The least correlated economies of Viet Nam and the Philippines plausibly reflect the unique events that these countries experienced over the sample period.

3.3.3 Changing Trade Patterns

Following the GFC, China is undoubtedly important for ASEAN6's business cycle. Dungey et al. (2018) find that China affects ASEAN business cycle via merchandise trade. In this section, we expand the analysis by decomposing the direct bilateral trade into intermediate goods, and consumption goods and explore to what extent China's influence on ASEAN6's business cycle penetrates through these two channels. The importance of these channels over time are also examined.

The selection of export weights is justified as follows: (i) As discussed in Chap. 1, exports in intermediate goods, and exports in consumption goods illustrate different mechanisms via which output shocks are transmitted across countries; (ii) These two trade flows represent different technological, cultural, political and other cross-border linkages such as foreign direct investment (FDI); (iii) The weights based on these two measures could also capture factors such as changes in tariffs and non-tariff restrictions, changes in transportation costs, exchange-rate movements and the ability to quantify the income competitive effects through third markets; (iv) Export weights are reasonably the most consistent among several assessable measures and the data are easily available (see also Abeysinghe and Forbes 2005; Dungey et al. 2018); and (v) The weights are appropriate since China's influence is the main focus of this chapter, and its expansion has affected the ASEAN economies dramatically *via* trade linkages rather than through financial linkages.

To measure bilateral trade flows of exports of intermediate goods, and consumption goods respectively, the following export shares are constructed for each economy included in our sample.

$$w_{ijt} = \frac{x_{ijt}}{x_{it}} \tag{3.1}$$

where the weights are exports (x_{ijt}) from country i to country j respectively divided by total exports (x_{it}) of country i at time t.

The export-weighted series for each economy are constructed as follows.

$$\sum_{j=1}^{n} w_{ijt} = w_{i1t} + w_{i2t} + \cdots + w_{int} = 1 \quad \text{where } i \neq j \tag{3.2}$$

where $i \neq j$; $j = 1, 2, \ldots, n$.

To reduce the noise in the series, the export weighted series are smoothed using the three-year moving average method.

Table 3.2 reports the regional export shares and regional export shares of intermediate goods and consumption goods of the ASEAN6 economies, respectively. From Table 3.2, it can be deduced that, in 2018, around 55% of ASEAN6's intermediate goods were exported to the other countries in the sample (ASEAN6 and non-ASEAN RCEP). If this is further decomposed, 20% of the intermediate exports were to the ASEAN6, while 15% were to China, and the remaining 20% were to the other non-ASEAN RCEP member countries. Amongst the ASEAN6, Indonesia had the highest intermediate export shares to the country sample, that is, around 70% followed by Malaysia with 60%. ASEAN6's intermediate exports to China had been rising rapidly from 3% in 1995 to 15% in 2018, indicating the rising importance of China in the region. In terms of intra-regional trade, Singapore and Malaysia commanded the largest share of intermediate exports to ASEAN, around 28% and 26% respectively. Except for Singapore and Viet Nam, the intra-regional intermediate goods trade of ASEAN6 did not vary much for the past 25 years. However, Viet Nam's intermediate exports to the region shrunk sharply from 32% in 1995 to only 10% in 2018, while Singapore's exports declined from 36% in 2005 to 28% in 2018.

As reported in the bottom panel of Table 3.2, in 2018, approximately 44% of ASEAN6's exports of consumption goods were to the country sample, and though the export shares to China were rising, the rate at which it was rising was lower compared to the shares of the intermediate goods. In terms of intra-regional trade, Viet Nam and the Philippines occupied the bottom positions as they had lower shares of consumption goods exports to ASEAN, around 5% and 7% respectively, while Singapore and Malaysia recorded the larger shares at 27% and 24% respectively. Overall, we can infer that the 12 countries are more integrated via the intermediate goods channel than through the consumption goods channel.

Figure 3.3 depicts some major changes in the export-shares of intermediate goods and consumption goods for China and ASEAN6 economies with the non-ASEAN RCEP countries for the 1995Q1 to 2018Q4 period. Explicitly, it illustrates how the export intensities of the ASEAN6, and China have evolved over time between the two export categories. The ASEAN6 economies' direct exports of intermediate goods to China have been rising and looks more prominent in the post-2005, while intermediate exports to Japan were on the decline. The intermediate export shares to China increased from 3% in 1995 to 15% in 2018 and since 2011, export shares to China were greater than that to Japan. This is not surprising as one of the key features of Chinese manufacturing exports is their reliance on foreign intermediate inputs. Two other important export destinations for ASEAN6's intermediate goods are South Korea and India, and in 2018, the export shares to these economies were around 4%. Though intermediate exports to India were rising from a share of hardly one percent in 1995 to 4% in 2018, it was still relatively small compared with the rapid growth in intermediate exports to China.

Even though Japan is still the leading export destination for ASEAN6's consumption goods, the export shares appear to be trending downward, shifting from 15% in 1995 to 10% in 2018 (see top right panel of Fig. 3.3). On the other hand, export shares to China were on an uptrend, rising from one percent in 1995 to 8% in 2018. The export shares to Australia and South Korea in 2018 were around 4% each. Overall, the

Table 3.2 ASEAN6 - regional export shares

ASEAN6	Exports to country sample[a]			Exports to ASEAN6			Exports to China		
	1995	2005	2018	1995	2005	2018	1995	2005	2018
Intermediate goods exports									
Indonesia	0.61	0.69	0.70	0.15	0.20	0.23	0.05	0.09	0.18
Malaysia	0.50	0.52	0.60	0.28	0.24	0.26	0.03	0.07	0.15
Philippines	0.36	0.53	0.48	0.16	0.18	0.17	0.02	0.11	0.13
Singapore	0.52	0.57	0.55	0.36	0.36	0.28	0.02	0.09	0.15
Thailand	0.49	0.53	0.54	0.27	0.22	0.20	0.03	0.11	0.14
Viet Nam	0.61	0.76	0.42	0.32	0.26	0.10	0.04	0.17	0.17
Average	0.52	0.60	0.55	0.26	0.24	0.20	0.03	0.11	0.15
Consumption goods exports									
Indonesia	0.34	0.24	0.39	0.12	0.10	0.20	0.01	0.01	0.06
Malaysia	0.37	0.38	0.47	0.21	0.23	0.27	0.01	0.02	0.05
Philippines	0.24	0.24	0.45	0.02	0.07	0.07	0.01	0.01	0.11
Singapore	0.39	0.46	0.55	0.20	0.26	0.24	0.01	0.05	0.08
Thailand	0.36	0.32	0.44	0.12	0.09	0.15	0.03	0.03	0.08
Viet Nam	0.38	0.26	0.34	0.15	0.06	0.05	0.02	0.03	0.10
Average	0.34	0.32	0.44	0.14	0.14	0.16	0.01	0.03	0.08

Note [a]Refers to the remaining countries of ASEAN6 and non-ASEAN RCEP
Source Compiled from UNCTADstat (2020)

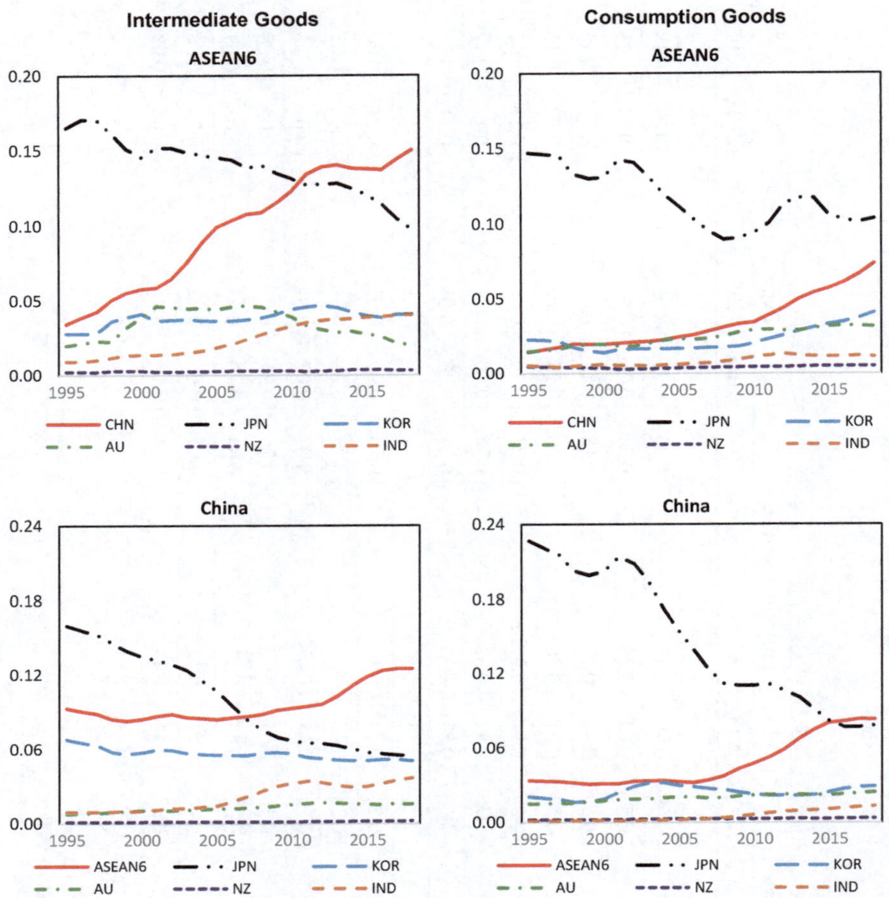

Fig. 3.3 ASEAN6-China—Export shares in intermediate goods and consumption goods, 1995–2018. *Notes* The vertical axis, export shares of intermediate goods and consumption goods, reflect changes in trade patterns of China and ASEAN6. See Table A.1 for country codes. *Source* Authors' own compilation

ASEAN6 economies relied heavily on intermediate goods compared to consumption goods for export expansion, and their main export destinations were China, Japan, and South Korea. The high dependence on the East Asian markets, particularly on China, increased the ASEAN6's exposure to any instabilities in those economies.

Rapid growth in China features strongly in the changing structure of international trade. Since 2005, the ASEAN6 economies were the main export destinations for China's intermediate goods compared to consumption goods (bottom left panel of Fig. 3.3). China's exports of intermediate goods to ASEAN6 increased from 9% in 1995 to 12% in 2018 and those to Japan declined from 18% to 5% respectively. Conversely, in 1995, around 23% of China's consumption goods exports were to

Japan, while only 3% was to ASEAN6. However, in 2018, China's export shares to both Japan and ASEAN6 were roughly at 8%. This shows, the bilateral trade integration between China and ASEAN6 had increased with time through both intermediate goods and consumption goods.

Figure 3.4 presents the export-shares of intermediate goods and consumption goods of the individual ASEAN6 economies to the non-ASEAN RCEP members. Each of the ASEAN6's exports of intermediate goods to China had surged dramatically over the period of review, whilst that of Japan had declined gradually over time. Amongst these, the export shares of the Philippines to China increased the least, while Japan was still its largest export destination. An increase of 10% was observed in Indonesia's intermediate exports to India, while gradual growth in exports of intermediate goods to South Korea from Indonesia, Viet Nam and the Philippines was noted.

As for consumption goods exports (right panel of Fig. 3.4), Japan was still the major destination for ASEAN6. Yet, the importance of its exports to each ASEAN6 had been gradually declining over the period of review. For many decades, Japan operated as a primary source of growth driver for ASEAN6, having emerged as a growth engine for the region from the mid-1960s, and subsequently developing intense trade-linkages with these emerging Asian economies. The economic interdependence between ASEAN6 and Japan, particularly Malaysia, Thailand and Indonesia increased in late 1980s, where Japanese firms transferred its production to these economies. After the AFC, the regional economic linkages of Japan waned, reflecting the reduction of its FDIs and bank lending (Dungey et al. 2018).

In the early 1980s, the ASEAN6 economies undertook significant structural reforms and shifted more towards regional demand as a primary source of growth. As reported in Table 3.2, between 1995 and 2018, on average the export shares of ASEAN6 economies to rest of the group members for intermediate goods had decreased from 26% to 20%, while for consumption goods, the shares increased slightly from 14% to 16%. As shown in Fig. 3.5, the proportion of ASEAN6's intermediate goods exports to Singapore appeared to be larger than the rest of the ASEAN members, although on average, its exports had declined during the period of review. Malaysia and Singapore seemed more integrated between them than with the other ASEAN members, while the Philippines and Viet Nam appeared less integrated with the ASEAN region. From an intra-ASEAN perspective, Thailand, and Indonesia displayed relatively higher degrees of integration with Malaysia and Singapore, than with the other ASEAN6 countries.

Overall, since 2005, the export shares of intermediate goods from Indonesia, the Philippines and Thailand to China were larger than the export shares to the other ASEAN members (see left panel of Fig. 3.5). Likewise, the strong bilateral ties between Singapore and Malaysia with China continued until 2010, after which the intermediate export share of these two nations to China tapered off. The three countries that have established trade ties with China, which are Malaysia, Singapore, and Thailand, are more integrated with the region through the intermediate goods channel. Two relevant explanations for this are: First, the three countries are lead players for intra-ASEAN trade and therefore have already established deep integrated trade ties

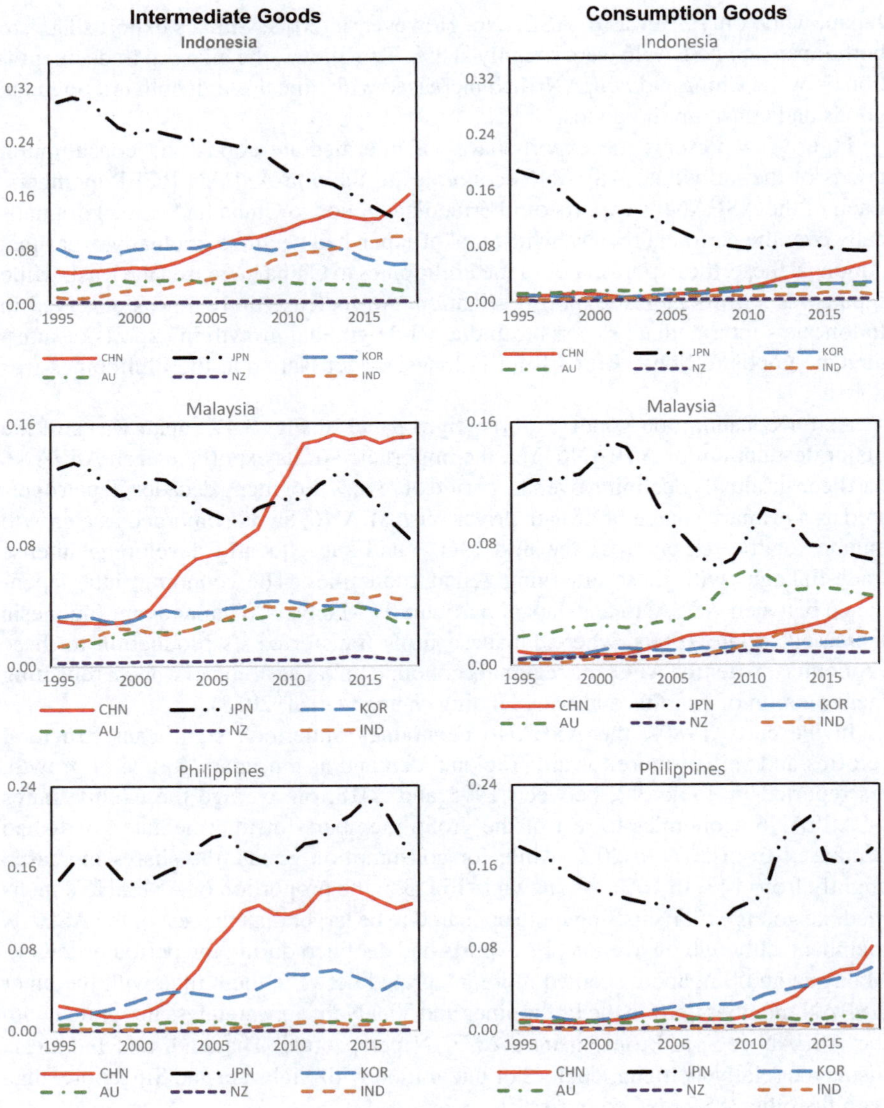

Fig. 3.4 ASEAN6—Export shares in intermediate goods and consumption goods to non-ASEAN RCEP, 1995–2018. *Notes* The vertical axis, the export shares of intermediate goods and consumption goods, indicate changes in trade patterns of the individual ASEAN6 countries. See Table A.1 for country codes. *Source* Authors' own compilation

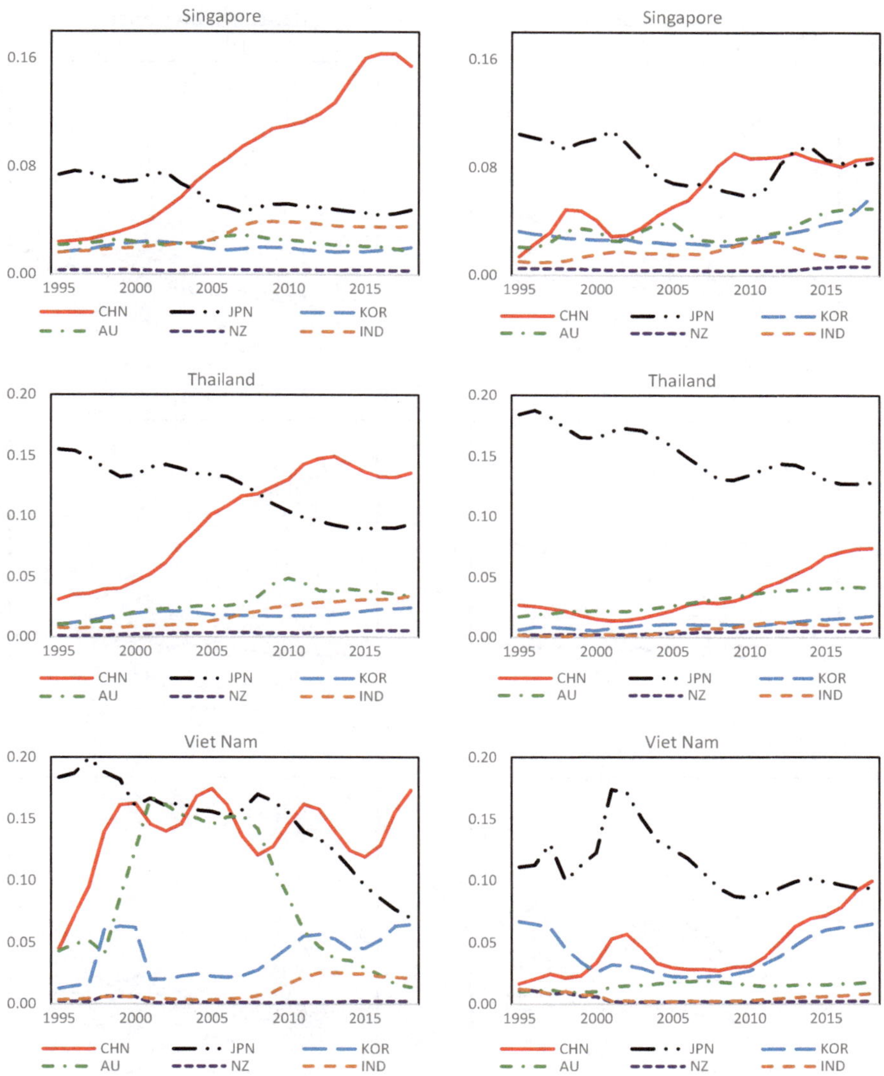

Fig. 3.4 (continued)

with the region. Second, Malaysia and Thailand may have plausibly avoided more disruptions in trade with China's positioning in the region as they have managed to maintain consistent trade surpluses with China (trade deficits from China's perspective; see Chap. 2), while the remaining ASEAN6 countries shifted from surpluses to deficits in trade with China.

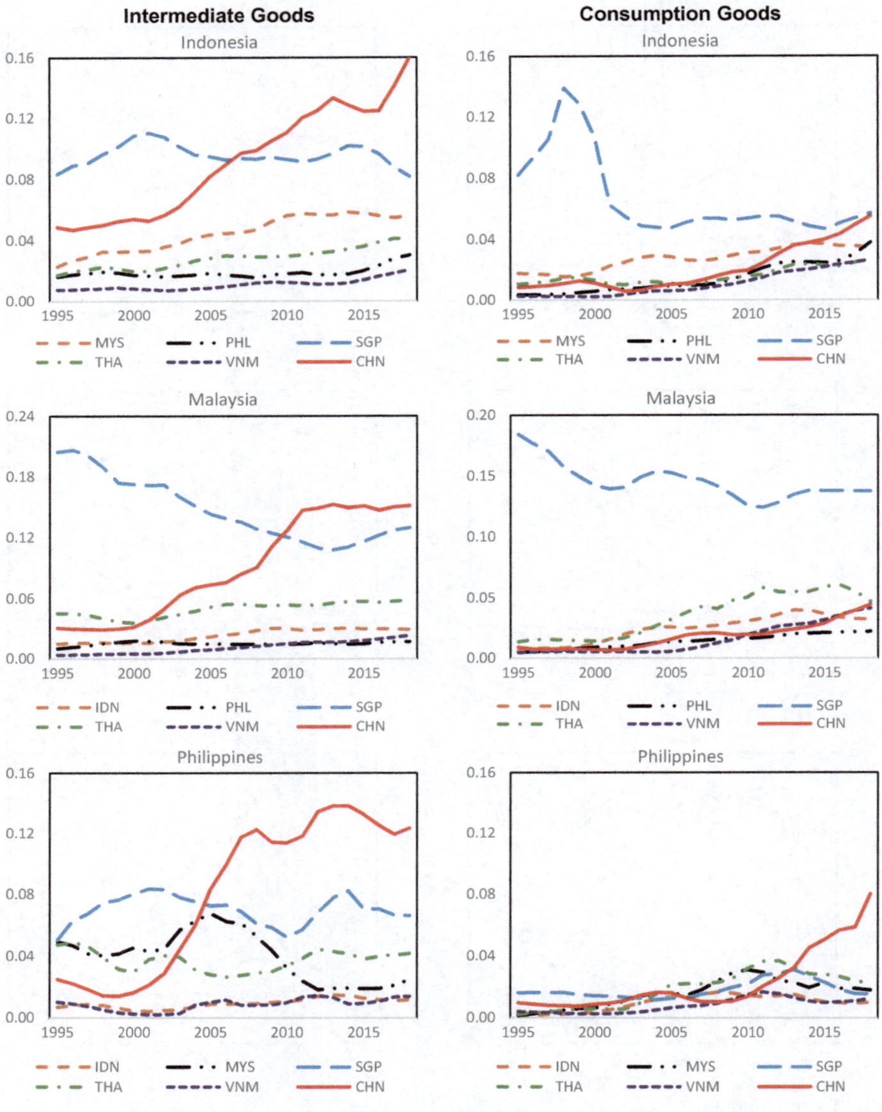

Fig. 3.5 ASEAN6—Export shares in intermediate goods and consumption goods to China and ASEAN6, 1995–2018. *Notes* The vertical axis, the export shares of intermediate goods and consumption goods, indicate changes in trade patterns of the individual ASEAN6 countries. See Table A.1 for country codes. *Source* Authors' own compilation

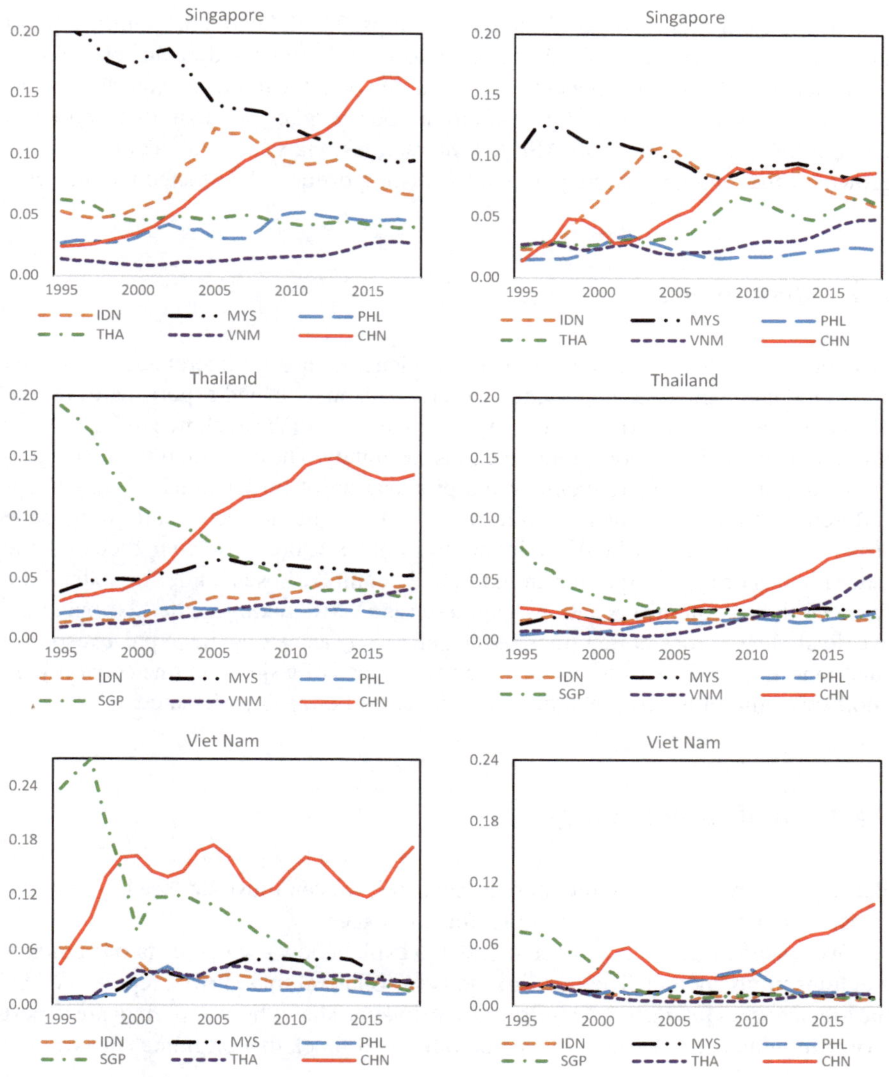

Fig. 3.5 (continued)

A different pattern emerged for the exports of consumption goods, based on the right panel of Fig. 3.5. Singapore was the largest export destination for consumption goods from both Malaysia and Indonesia, though the export shares in Indonesia fell sharply from 14% in 1998 to 5% in 2005, while for Malaysia, the uptrend in export shares continued. Since 2010, the exports of consumption goods of the Philippines, Thailand, and Viet Nam destined to China surpassed that to other ASEAN members.

The trends in export shares observed from Figs. 3.3, 3.4 and 3.5, overall, support the observations made in Chap. 2, in that, trade is a relevant and dynamic channel for the China-ASEAN engagement. Notwithstanding that, the trends in exports of intermediate goods, and exports of consumption goods suggest an additional influence on ASEAN6, that is, the intra-ASEAN interactions, via which the evolution in the growth of the regional trading partners has disproportionately affected the former.

3.4 Methodology

To capture both direct and indirect interdependencies via multilateral trade-links, the VAR model is estimated, employing quarterly data on GDP and export shares for the 12 economies. We construct a time varying trade matrix (W) as shown in Eq. 3.1, for intermediate goods and consumption goods separately. The construction of changing trade weights allows us to examine the propagation of international shocks under different configurations of international trade links due to the transforming trade structure over time. As in Abeysinghe and Forbes (2005), we first focus on the determinants of total output for an individual country. Subsequently, we extend the framework to a system of equations, expressed as a VAR, linking all the 12 economies. We illustrate the cross-border transmission effects by analyzing the impulse response functions as it enables us to disentangle the impacts of a shock in one economy on another, highlighting the prevailing bilateral cross-border interdependencies.

3.4.1 Modelling Strategy

Based on our review of the literature in Sect. 3.2, we can illustrate (see Fig. 3.6) the transmission of output shocks through trade linkages.

Two specific trade linkages can be used to explain how a shock from one country can transmit to another. The first linkage is via bilateral trade flows, represented by the green arrows in Fig. 3.6. This direct trade linkage shows how important are export shares in influencing a country's vulnerability to a shock that originates in a trading

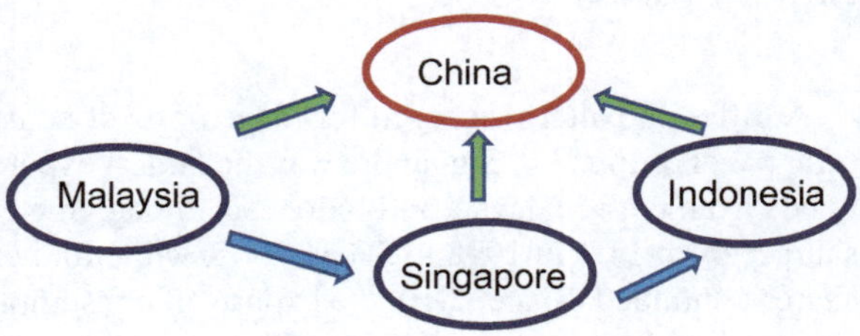

Fig. 3.6 Transmission of output shocks. *Source* Authors' own illustration

partner. For example, it measures how each ASEAN6 members' exports to China are affected by a shock that originates in China.

As revealed in the trade literature, though the bilateral-trade flows are important determinants of an economy's vulnerability to a foreign shock, it can only explain a small portion of the effects. The second important linkage is the indirect effect, represented by the blue arrows in Fig. 3.6. The indirect effects capture the impact of one country on another via its influence on the output growth of its trading partners—through supply chains and third markets. For example, a shock or slower growth in China not only affects exports of Malaysia but also affects exports of Singapore and Indonesia. This, in turn, reduces growth in these economies and the demand for the exports between them, and from other economies. Therefore, a shock that originates in China can have multiplier effects through multilateral trade chains and income effects on output and growth in other economies. The effects from these indirect trade linkages are important and can transmit shocks through very different patterns than predicted by direct, bilateral trade flows. Therefore, a country-specific shock can lead to strong and prolonged fluctuations because its initial impact can be amplified by feedback effects operating through the trade channels. Indirect effects also mean that shocks in one country can affect other countries and regions despite weak direct trade linkages.

To capture the effects of direct and indirect trade (see Chap. 1 for the definition) linkage, we develop a model simultaneously equating output supply and demand linking the 12 economies. As in Abeysinghe and Forbes (2005), we begin by focusing on the determinants of total output (Y_i) for an individual country i. Since we are first focusing only on one country, we will drop the subscript i and write a country's output as follows:

$$Y_t = Y_{NX,t} + X_t \tag{3.3}$$

where $Y_{NX,t}$ and X_t are non-export and export components of output respectively at a given time t. The total exports can be expressed as the sum of exports of country i to all its trading partners:

$$X_t = X_{1,t} + X_{2,t} + \cdots + X_{n,t} \quad \text{where } j = 1, 2, \ldots, n;$$

and can be summarized as

$$X_t = \sum_{j=1}^{n} X_{j,t} \tag{3.4}$$

and by inserting (3.4) into (3.3), yields:

$$Y_t = Y_{NX,t} + \sum_{j=1}^{n} X_{j,t} \tag{3.5}$$

Equation (3.5) can be represented in terms of growth rates:

$$\frac{dY_t}{Y_t} = \frac{1}{Y_t}\left[dY_{NX,t} + \sum_{j=1}^{n} dX_{j,t}\right] \tag{3.6}$$

Country i's export to country j is assumed to be a reduced form function of output in country j and hence the changes in country i's export to country j can be shown as follows:

$$dX_{j,t} = \left(\frac{\partial X_{j,t}}{\partial Y_{j,t}}\right) dY_{j,t} \tag{3.7}$$

and by inserting (3.7) into (3.6), yields:

$$\frac{dY_t}{Y_t} = \frac{1}{Y_t} dY_{NX,t} + \frac{1}{Y_t}\left[\sum_{j=1}^{n}\left(\frac{\partial X_{j,t}}{\partial Y_{j,t}}\right) dY_{j,t}\right] \tag{3.8}$$

where the second term in the right-hand side is represented as

$$\frac{dX_t}{Y_t} = \frac{1}{Y_t}\left[\sum_{j=1}^{n}\left(\frac{\partial X_{j,t}}{\partial Y_{j,t}}\right) dY_{j,t}\right] \tag{3.9}$$

and by rearranging the terms in (3.9) yields:

$$\frac{dX_t}{Y_t} = \frac{X_t}{Y_t}\left[\sum_{j=1}^{n}\left(\frac{\partial X_{j,t}}{\partial Y_{j,t}}\right)\left(\frac{Y_{j,t}}{X_{j,t}}\right)\left(\frac{X_{j,t}}{X_t}\right)\left(\frac{dY_{j,t}}{Y_{j,t}}\right)\right] \tag{3.10}$$

and can be simplified as

$$\frac{dX_t}{Y_t} = \frac{X_t}{Y_t}\left[\sum_{j=1}^{n} \eta_j \omega_{j,t} y_{j,t}\right] \tag{3.11}$$

where

- $\eta_j = \left(\frac{\partial X_{j,t}}{\partial Y_{j,t}}\right)\left(\frac{Y_{j,t}}{X_{j,t}}\right)$ is the income elasticity of exports of country i with respect to country j's income,
- $\omega_{j,t} = \left(\frac{X_{j,t}}{X_t}\right)$ represents export shares of country i with country j at time t and,
- $y_{j,t} = \left(\frac{dY_{j,t}}{Y_{j,t}}\right)$ represents country j's growth rate at time t.

We assume that income elasticities are equal across countries, consistent with the assumption underlying most aggregate export-demand equations. As a result,

$$\eta_j = \eta \quad \text{where } j = 1, 2, \ldots, n$$

and Eq. (3.11) can be simplified further:

$$\frac{dX_t}{Y_t} = \alpha y_t^f \tag{3.12}$$

where

$$\alpha = \eta \frac{X_t}{Y_t} \quad \text{while } y_t^f = \sum_{j=1}^{n} \omega_{j,t} y_{j,t}$$

and using lower-case letters to indicate growth rates and inserting (3.12), Eq. (3.8) can be written for country i as follows:

$$y_{it} = \alpha_i y_{it}^f + \upsilon_t \tag{3.13}$$

The right-hand side of Eq. (3.13) represents the time varying export-share weighted average of output growth rates and α_i measures the change in country i's growth, given a change in external demand for exports and is assumed to be constant. υ_t captures any omitted variables not included in the model.

If output growth in every country j is exogenous to output growth in country i, then Eq. (3.13) would capture the direct impact of a shock in country j on country i. As discussed in the earlier part of this section, we highlighted the importance of the indirect multiplier effect of the shock through other countries. The output growth in every country j is therefore not exogenous to output growth in every other country i. To capture the direct and indirect effects, the GDP growth, Eq. (3.13) for each country in our sample can be expressed as an autoregressive distributed lag model with white noise errors:

$$y_{it} = \lambda_i + \sum_{k=1}^{p} \phi_{ki} y_{it-k} + \sum_{k=0}^{p} \beta_{ki} y_{it-k}^f + \varepsilon_{i,t} \tag{3.14}$$

where $y_{it}^f = \sum_{j=1}^{n} \omega_{ij,t} y_{j,t}$ and $w_{ij,t} = \frac{x_{ij,t}}{x_{i,t}}$ is the export share from country i to country j over the total exports of country i.

Assume there are three countries ($n = 3$) and one lag ($p = 1$) and the system of equations is formed by estimating Eq. (3.14) for each country as follows.

$$\begin{aligned} y_{1t} &= \lambda_1 + \phi_{11} y_{1t-1} + \beta_{01}[\omega_{12t} y_{2t} + \omega_{13t} y_{3t}] \\ &\quad + \beta_{11}\left[\omega_{12t-1} y_{2t-1} + \omega_{13t-1} y_{3t-1}\right] + \varepsilon_{1t}, \end{aligned}$$

$$y_{2t} = \lambda_2 + \phi_{22} y_{2t-1} + \beta_{02}[\omega_{21t} y_{1t} + \omega_{23t} y_{3t}] \\ + \beta_{12}\left[\omega_{21t-1} y_{1t-1} + \omega_{23t-1} y_{3t-1}\right] + \varepsilon_{2t},$$

$$y_{3t} = \lambda_3 + \phi_{33} y_{3t-1} + \beta_{03}[\omega_{31t} y_{1t} + \omega_{32t} y_{2t}] \\ + \beta_{13}[\omega_{31t-1} y_{1t-1} + \omega_{32t-1} y_{2t-1}] + \varepsilon_{3t},$$

Rewriting the above equations:

$$y_{1t} - \beta_{01}\omega_{12t} y_{2t} - \beta_{01}\omega_{13t} y_{3t} \\ = \lambda_1 + \phi_{11} y_{1t-1} + \beta_{11}\omega_{12t-1} y_{2t-1} + \beta_{11}\omega_{13t-1} y_{3t-1} + \varepsilon_{1t}$$

$$y_{2t} - \beta_{02}\omega_{21t} y_{1t} - \beta_{02}\omega_{23t} y_{3t} \\ = \lambda_2 + \phi_{22} y_{2t-1} + \beta_{12}\omega_{21t-1} y_{1t-1} + \beta_{12}\omega_{23t-1} y_{3t-1} + \varepsilon_{2t}$$

$$y_{3t} - \beta_{03}\omega_{31t} y_{1t} - \beta_{03}\omega_{32t} y_{2t} \\ = \lambda_3 + \phi_{33} y_{3t-1} + \beta_{13}\omega_{31t-1} y_{1t-1} + \beta_{13}\omega_{32t-1} y_{2t-1} + \varepsilon_{3t}$$

And expressed in a matrix form as:

$$\begin{bmatrix} 1 & -\beta_{01}\omega_{12t} & -\beta_{01}\omega_{13t} \\ -\beta_{02}\omega_{21t} & 1 & -\beta_{02}\omega_{23t} \\ -\beta_{03}\omega_{31t} & -\beta_{03}\omega_{32t} & 1 \end{bmatrix} \begin{bmatrix} y_{1t} \\ y_{2t} \\ y_{3t} \end{bmatrix} \\ = \begin{bmatrix} \lambda_1 \\ \lambda_2 \\ \lambda_3 \end{bmatrix} + \begin{bmatrix} \phi_{11} & \beta_{11}\omega_{12t-1} & \beta_{11}\omega_{13t-1} \\ \beta_{12}\omega_{21t-1} & \phi_{22} & \beta_{12}\omega_{23t-1} \\ \beta_{13}\omega_{31t-1} & \beta_{13}\omega_{32t-1} & \phi_{33} \end{bmatrix} \begin{bmatrix} y_{1t-1} \\ y_{2t-1} \\ y_{3t-1} \end{bmatrix} + \begin{bmatrix} \varepsilon_{1t} \\ \varepsilon_{2t} \\ \varepsilon_{3t} \end{bmatrix} \tag{3.15}$$

Equation (3.15) can be written more compactly as a VAR representation.

$$(\mathrm{B}_0 * \boldsymbol{W}_t)\boldsymbol{y}_t = \boldsymbol{\lambda} + (\mathrm{B}_1 * \boldsymbol{W}_{t-1})\boldsymbol{y}_{t-1} + \boldsymbol{\varepsilon}_t \tag{3.16}$$

where

$$\mathrm{B}_0 = \begin{bmatrix} 1 & -\beta_{01} & -\beta_{01} \\ -\beta_{02} & 1 & -\beta_{02} \\ -\beta_{03} & -\beta_{03} & 1 \end{bmatrix}, \quad \mathrm{B}_1 = \begin{bmatrix} \phi_{11} & \beta_{11} & \beta_{11} \\ \beta_{12} & \phi_{22} & \beta_{12} \\ \beta_{13} & \beta_{13} & \phi_{22} \end{bmatrix},$$

$$\mathbf{W}_{t-p} = \begin{bmatrix} 1 & \omega_{12t-p} & \omega_{13t-p} \\ \omega_{21t-p} & 1 & \omega_{23t-p} \\ \omega_{31t-p} & \omega_{32t-p} & 1 \end{bmatrix} \text{for } p = 0, 1.$$

The above VAR formulation is useful for the purpose of estimating the direct and indirect trade linkages and for the impulse-response analysis.

3.4.2 VAR Framework

The system of equations is formed by estimating Eq. (3.14) for each of the 12 countries ($n = 12$) and the general VAR (p) for the entire system is expressed as follows:

$$(\mathrm{B}_0 * \boldsymbol{W}_t)\boldsymbol{y}_t = \boldsymbol{\lambda} + (\mathrm{B}_1 * \boldsymbol{W}_{t-1})\boldsymbol{y}_{t-1} + \cdots + (\mathrm{B}_p * \boldsymbol{W}_{t-p})\boldsymbol{y}_{t-p} + \boldsymbol{\varepsilon}_t \tag{3.17}$$

where $\boldsymbol{y}_t$ is (12 × 1) vector of countries' output at time t, while $\boldsymbol{\lambda}$ is the (12 × 1) vector of constants, and $\boldsymbol{\varepsilon}_t$ is the (12 × 1) vector of white noise.

$\boldsymbol{B}$ and $\boldsymbol{W}$ are (12 × 12) matrices of parameter and export share matrices respectively, while $*$ is the elementwise product of two matrices and (p) represents the lag structure. $(\mathrm{B}_p * \boldsymbol{W}_{t-p})$ includes the effective parameter matrices, which are allowed to change due to changes in the export-weight matrix over time.

We compute impulse responses to illustrate how a shock to an individual country has a direct and indirect influence on other countries in the sample through trade-links and output-multiplier effects. We can use the trade-weighting matrix ($\mathbf{W}_t$) at any point in time and generate the impulse responses at a desired time. For a given $\boldsymbol{W}$-matrix, the reduced form Eq. (3.17) can be expressed as:

$$\boldsymbol{y}_t = \boldsymbol{\delta} + \boldsymbol{\Phi}_1\boldsymbol{y}_{t-1} + \boldsymbol{\Phi}_2\boldsymbol{y}_{t-2} + \cdots + \boldsymbol{\Phi}_p\boldsymbol{y}_{t-p} + \boldsymbol{\upsilon}_t \tag{3.18}$$

where $\boldsymbol{\Phi}_i = (\boldsymbol{B}_0 * \boldsymbol{W})^{-1}(\boldsymbol{B}_i * \boldsymbol{W}), i = 1, \ldots, p$ and $\boldsymbol{\upsilon}_t = (\boldsymbol{B}_0 * \boldsymbol{W})^{-1}\boldsymbol{\varepsilon}_t$.

Equation (3.18) can be summarized as

$$\boldsymbol{\Phi}(\boldsymbol{L})\boldsymbol{y}_t = \boldsymbol{\upsilon}_t \tag{3.19}$$

where $\boldsymbol{\Phi}(\boldsymbol{L}) = \boldsymbol{I}_n - \boldsymbol{\Phi}_1(\boldsymbol{L}) - \boldsymbol{\Phi}_2(\boldsymbol{L})^2 - \cdots - \boldsymbol{\Phi}_p(\boldsymbol{L})^p$.

To compute the impulse responses, we convert Eq. (3.19) into moving-average as follows.

$$\boldsymbol{y}_t = \boldsymbol{\Psi}(\boldsymbol{L})\boldsymbol{\upsilon}_t \tag{3.20}$$

and $\boldsymbol{\Psi}(\boldsymbol{L}) = \boldsymbol{\Phi}(\boldsymbol{L})^{-1}$. Therefore, Eq. (3.20) can be written as

$$\boldsymbol{y}_t = \sum_{k=0}^{\infty} \boldsymbol{\Psi}_k\boldsymbol{\upsilon}_{t-k} = \sum_{k=0}^{\infty} \boldsymbol{\Psi}_k(\boldsymbol{B}_0 * \boldsymbol{W})^{-1}\boldsymbol{\varepsilon}_{t-k} \tag{3.21}$$

where $\boldsymbol{\Psi}_0 = \boldsymbol{I}, \boldsymbol{\Psi}_k = \sum_{m=1}^{k} \boldsymbol{\Phi}_m \boldsymbol{\Psi}_{k-m}, k = 1, 2, \ldots$

It is important to note that the output shocks that we investigate in this chapter are not structural. Since the focus of our study is to assess the transmission of output shocks across countries, we use the VAR framework described in Eq. (3.17) to identify the country-specific shocks by conditioning each variable on contemporaneous values of foreign-specific variables, which reduces the cross-country dependence of the shocks.[21] This methodological approach enables us to report impulse response functions while maintaining a parsimonious model specification across the entire period. This approach also enables us to examine the impact of output shocks with alternative configurations of cross-country linkages.

In our analysis to capture changes in trade-induced macroeconomic links, two different export-weight matrices are considered, one to represent the export shares of intermediate goods, while the other is to represent the export shares of consumption goods. This allows us to:

(i) Capture the changes in transmissions due to altering trade structures over the sample period for the two broad categories of exports;
(ii) Investigate how the transmission of shocks has changed after the emergence of China in the world economy. Specifically, we generate output shocks, using trade weights at different points in time, thus describing the fundamental aspect of China's rapidly changing role in the ASEAN region. Here, we concur with Cesa-Bianchi et al. (2012), that the response to an output shock depends on the choice of weights, even if similar parameter estimates are obtained using different weights matrix. This is an important consideration for this chapter, where the focus is on examining the possible effects of changing trade linkages between ASEAN6 with the non-ASEAN RCEP countries.
(iii) Employ the time-varying export weights, which are essential in our analysis, as they facilitate us to account for the development of trade relations among the 12 countries, which in turn allows for counterfactual simulation exercises. This methodological approach is vital as it allows us to consider the fact that trade integration has progressed over time with the acceleration of globalization in the mid-1990s.

3.5 Empirical Results

In this section we present the impulse responses for the ASEAN6 economies. We also provide the output multipliers to demonstrate the dynamic nature of the transmission mechanism and illustrate the international effects of a country-specific shock over time. Finally, we show the output growth co-movements within the ASEAN6 economies, along with the significance of both the direct and indirect effects.

To quantify the change in the transmission of external shocks to ASEAN6 and the emergence of China as a significant trading partner within the other non-ASEAN RCEP sub-group, we conduct a set of counterfactual simulation exercises using the VAR described in Section 3.4. In the first stage, using the time-varying export weights to construct foreign variables, we estimate the VAR model for the period 1995Q1 to 2018Q4. We use the two-stage least squares (2SLS) method to estimate, where we set $p = 1$, and utilize two lags $(y_{i,t-1}, y_{i,t-2})$ for each $y_{i,t}$ $(i = 1, \ldots, 12)$ as instruments. This approach is only possible because of the assumption that the growth rates in all the sample economies apart from i, are treated as a trade weighted variable and not as single independent variables. The use of 2SLS is warranted as y_{it}^{f} is endogenous. As a robustness check, we also estimate the model via the ordinary least squares (OLS) method but did not find qualitatively substantial differences in the results between the two estimation methods.

In the second stage, with the assumption that the estimated parameters are stable over time, we use the estimated VAR model to carry out counterfactual exercise for alternative trade matrices. We use trade weights for the years 2000, 2005, 2010 and 2018 and then we compare the resulting time responses of the transmission of specific output shocks across different counterfactual trade linkages. For instance, the impulse responses for a shock from China show how it affects the ASEAN6 on impact (first-round direct effects) and over time (second and higher-order indirect effects) for a given weighted trade matrix. By focusing on these four sets of trade weights, we can quantify how changes in non-ASEAN RCEP members trade patterns have altered the impact and transmission of shocks to ASEAN6, extracting from any indirect changes to parameter estimates that might have taken place because of changing trade weights. As we saw in Sect. 3.3, the most marked shift in trade weights were observed between 2000 to 2005, while the trade weights were relatively stable over the period 2005 to 2018. In the analysis of the international transmission of these shocks, we look at both regional and country-specific responses. The regional responses are constructed as weighted averages of the country specific responses.

3.5.1 ASEAN6 Impulse Responses

Figure 3.7 presents the cumulative impulse responses of ASEAN6 as a group, for 20 quarters due to a one-unit shock originating from China and other RCEP economies for the different weights of intermediate goods (left panel), and consumption goods (right panel) respectively. We assessed the responses for the different weight matrices—2000, 2005, 2010 and 2018—and the figures clearly show that impulse responses changed as we used different weights. In Fig. 3.7, in addition to focusing on output shock from China, we also assessed the shocks from Japan, South Korea, Australia, New Zealand and India, as shocks form the latter economies provide a natural benchmark against which to contrast the results for China on the remaining economies in the sample.

For the models estimated using the intermediate goods export weights (left panel of Fig. 3.7), the responses of ASEAN6 as a group to the shocks from China were the largest, followed by South Korea and Japan. Though the bilateral intermediate export shares of ASEAN6 to Japan were greater than South Korea (refer to Fig. 3.3), the effects of shocks from South Korea on ASEAN6 were larger compared to Japan. This

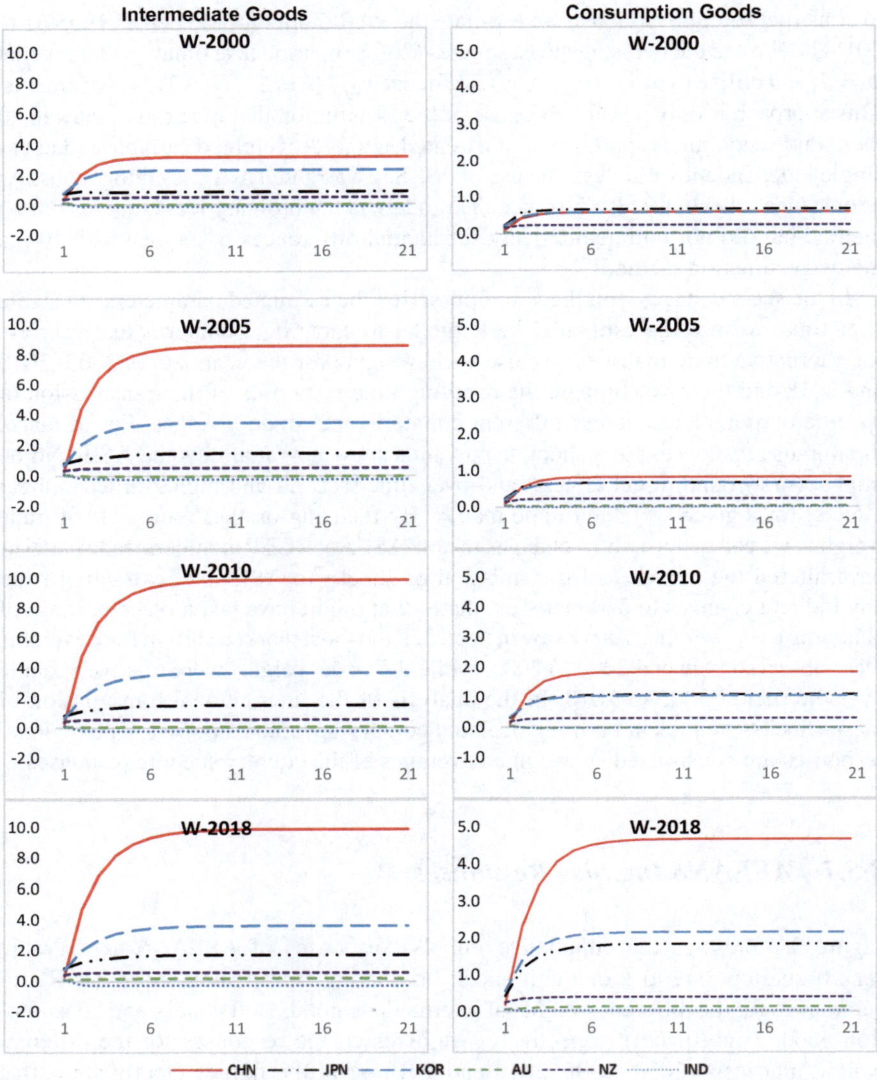

Fig. 3.7 Cumulative impulse responses of ASEAN6 to non-ASEAN RCEP, with different weights of intermediate goods and consumption goods. *Notes* The horizontal axis represents quarters, while the vertical axis shows the cumulative response to a one-unit output shock in the non-ASEAN RCEP members with different weights of intermediate goods, and consumption goods respectively. See Table A.1 for country codes. *Source* Authors' own estimation

could be associated with the indirect trade linkages discussed under Sect. 3.4.1, in that shocks transmit through very different patterns than predicted by direct flows. With more recent trade weights, a China output shock matters much more for ASEAN6, for example with 2005 weights, the responses of ASEAN6 increased by three times compared with 2000 weights. In the case of Japan, the opposite held true. The effects of a shock from Japan on ASEAN6 were less pronounced using recent intermediate trade weights, despite Japan's strong bilateral trade relationship with the ASEAN6. India, whose trade integration with the remaining economies in the sample was mainly driven by trade in services, had almost no impact on the ASEAN6 economies.

As for consumption goods export (right panel of Fig. 3.7), the responses of the ASEAN6 to the externally generated one-unit shocks were smaller than those for intermediate goods; it was almost four times smaller with 2000, 2005 and 2010 weights. It also followed a slightly different response to shocks originating from the non-ASEAN RCEP countries. Here, responses to China, Japan and South Korea were found to be similar using the 2000 and 2005 weights. A significant jump in response to the Chinese shock was observed for the 2018 weight, where the response was around eight, six and three times larger compared to responses to shocks generated using 2000, 2005 and 2010 weights, respectively. This highlights the rising importance of Chinese output shock transmissions to ASEAN6 economies via the consumption goods trade channel. Though the bilateral export shares of consumption goods of ASEAN6 to Japan were greater than China (refer to Fig. 3.3), the effects of shock from China appeared larger compared to Japan, highlighting again the importance of the indirect trade linkages that work through the third markets.

In general, we observed that the ASEAN6 economies were less sensitive to shocks in Australia, New Zealand, and India, compared to shocks originating from the three East Asian economies (China, Japan, and South Korea). As the trading sector of ASEAN6 had been the key source of its growth, it is plausible that it had been influenced by international transmissions via trade with East Asia. The output shocks that penetrated through the intermediate trade channel were more important compared to that penetrating through the consumption trade channel.

Since China plays an important role in the ASEAN6, we further explored the responses of the individual ASEAN6 economies to output shocks originating from China for the four trade weights mentioned above. Figure 3.8 displays those results. As shown in Fig. 3.8, except for Viet Nam, a China output shock mattered more for ASEAN6, using 2010 and 2018 intermediate trade weights. For instance, the impact of the Chinese output shock on Thailand with 2010 weights had increased the latter's responses by about four times compared to the 2000 weights, while for Viet Nam, the changes in the transmission of a China output shocks was notable with the 2018 weights. The ASEAN6 exhibited the same pattern, with progressive increases in responses to a Chinese output shock when using more recent consumption trade weights. The differences between the 2000 and 2018 responses were found to be quantitatively large.

We interpret this evidence as suggesting that both direct and indirect effects contribute to the stronger impact of a China output shock on ASEAN countries, and the indirect channel of transmission is at least as important as the more obvious

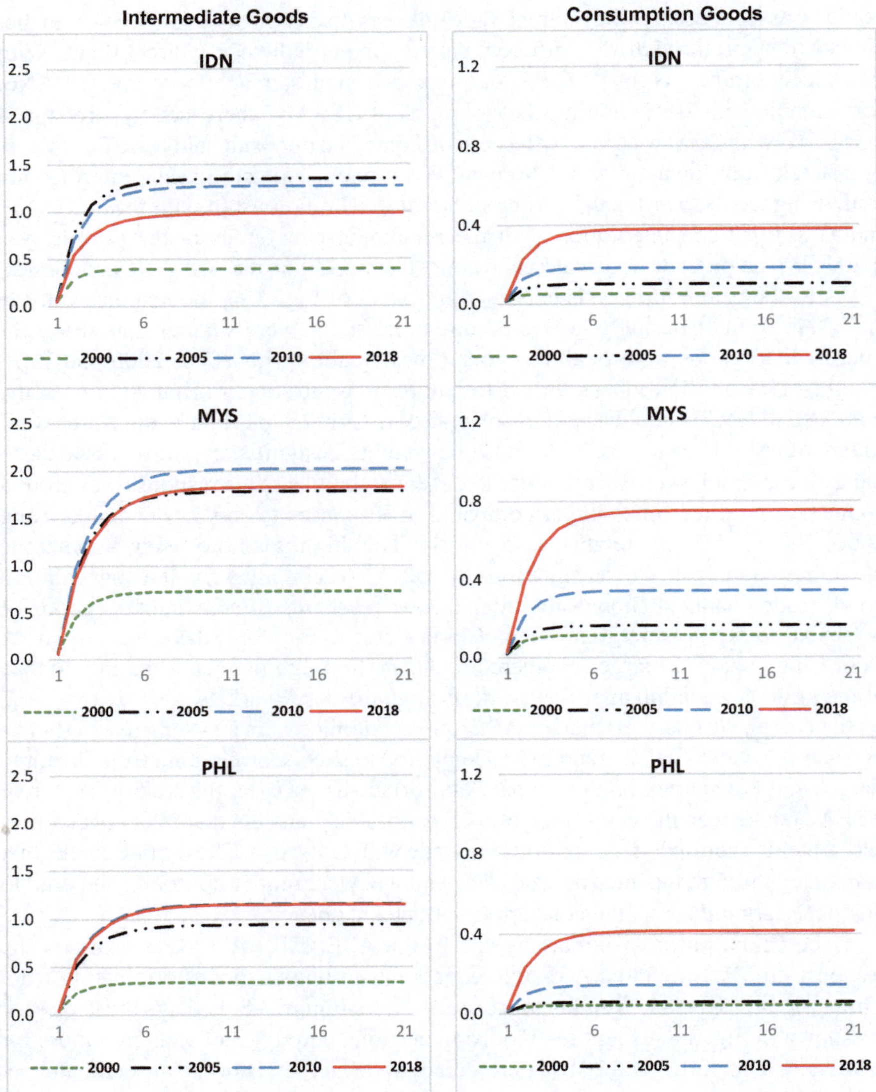

Fig. 3.8 Cumulative impulse responses of ASEAN6 to China, with different weights of intermediate and consumption goods. *Notes* The horizontal axis represents quarters, while the vertical axis shows the cumulative response to a one-unit output shock in China with different weights of intermediate goods, and consumption goods respectively. See Table A.1 for country codes. *Source* Authors' own estimation

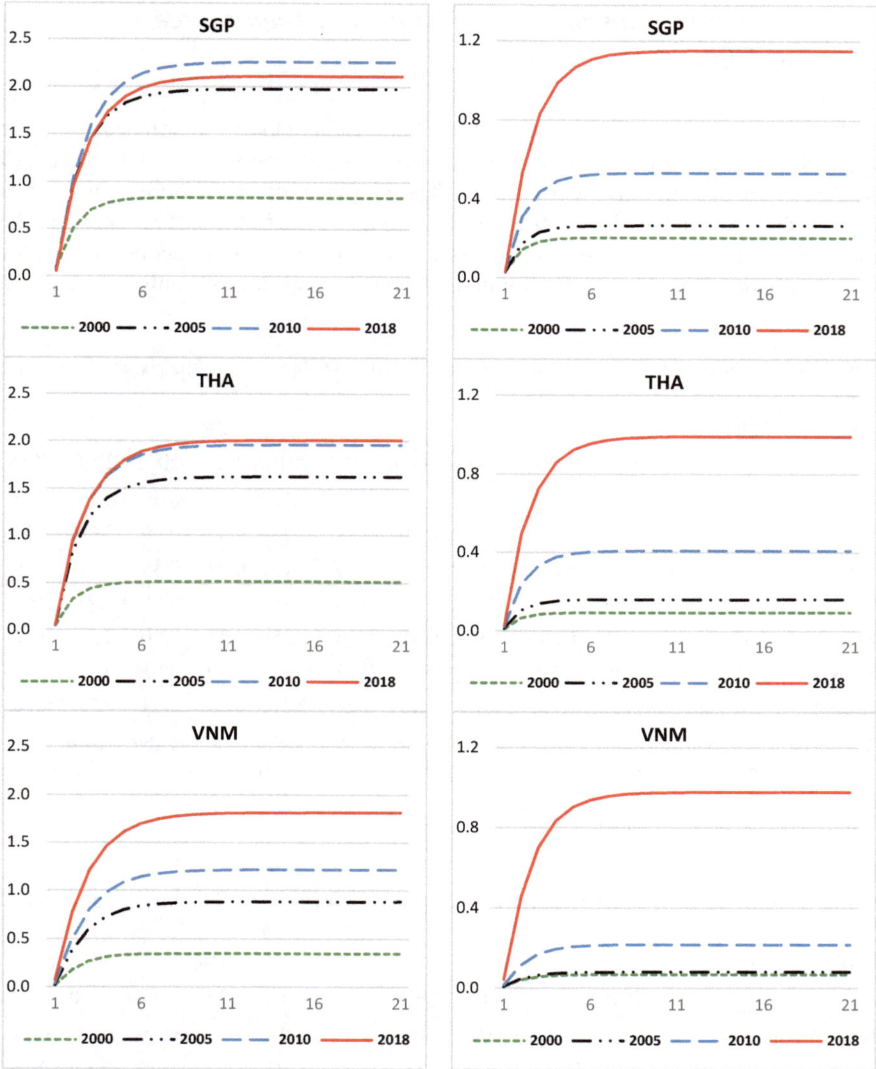

Fig. 3.8 (continued)

direct links. This is clear evidence that, the shifts in trade linkages between China, ASEAN6 and the rest of the non-ASEAN RCEP are affecting the region not only via stronger direct trade linkages but also through stronger ties between China and ASEAN6's traditional trading partners in the region. An important implication of this result is that other countries in the region, such as Japan and South Korea, may now be more affected by China through the increased impact of China's output shock on the ASEAN6 economies.

3.5.2 Dynamic Transmission Mechanism: Importance of China

Tables 3.3 and 3.4 report the output multipliers for shocks from China, Japan, and South Korea as these three economies were found to be important growth drivers of the ASEAN6 over the last two decades. The output multipliers were estimated as the cumulative impulse responses to external shocks after four quarters, showing the accumulated impact of a one-unit expansion in the GDP of driver economies on the output growth of the ASEAN6 economies. Table 3.3 captures not only how a shock

Table 3.3 Accumulated impact of growth drivers on ASEAN6, based on W-matrix of intermediate goods

ASEAN6	CHN				JPN				KOR			
	2000	2005	2010	2018	2000	2005	2010	2018	2000	2005	2010	2018
IDN	0.39	1.27	1.19	0.91	−0.06	0.08	0.07	0.12	0.27	0.50	0.43	0.35
MYS	0.71	1.65	1.83	1.64	0.22	0.30	0.28	0.28	0.56	0.69	0.69	0.59
PHL	0.33	0.88	1.05	1.04	0.09	0.14	0.15	0.15	0.27	0.38	0.41	0.39
SGP	0.81	1.82	2.05	1.89	0.27	0.32	0.33	0.33	0.61	0.75	0.77	0.65
THA	0.50	1.50	1.77	1.80	0.18	0.35	0.36	0.38	0.34	0.60	0.64	0.62
VNM	0.33	0.80	1.08	1.61	0.12	0.19	0.22	0.35	0.20	0.31	0.42	0.74
Average	0.51	1.32	1.50	1.48	0.14	0.23	0.24	0.27	0.38	0.54	0.56	0.56

Notes The rows indicate the responses of ASEAN6 to shocks that arise in the growth driver economies (China, Japan, and South Korea), as given in the columns. See Table A.1 for country codes
Source Authors' own estimation

Table 3.4 Accumulated impact of growth drivers on ASEAN6, based on W-matrix of consumption goods

ASEAN6	CHN				JPN				KOR			
	2000	2005	2010	2018	2000	2005	2010	2018	2000	2005	2010	2018
IDN	0.05	0.10	0.18	0.36	−0.04	−0.00	0.06	0.12	0.07	0.09	0.11	0.19
MYS	0.11	0.16	0.34	0.70	0.10	0.11	0.17	0.26	0.11	0.12	0.17	0.30
PHL	0.04	0.06	0.14	0.39	0.02	0.02	0.05	0.11	0.05	0.05	0.08	0.18
SGP	0.20	0.26	0.52	1.07	0.27	0.23	0.32	0.44	0.19	0.19	0.26	0.47
THA	0.10	0.16	0.40	0.92	0.20	0.22	0.30	0.42	0.09	0.13	0.21	0.40
VNM	0.07	0.08	0.21	0.91	0.10	0.09	0.16	0.41	0.07	0.09	0.17	0.53
Average	0.09	0.13	0.29	0.72	0.10	0.11	0.17	0.29	0.09	0.11	0.16	0.34

Notes The rows indicate the responses of ASEAN6 to shocks that arise in the growth driver economies (China, Japan, and South Korea), as given in the columns. See Table A.1 for country codes
Source Authors' own estimation

to the three growth driver economies directly effects the ASEAN6 economies, but also how the initial shock to one economy spreads through a chain of output effects in other countries. We find that the multiplier effects portrayed a different picture of the transmission of shocks than that provided by the bilateral trade flows between the RCEP economies.

From Table 3.3, we can clearly see that the propagation patterns by which the ASEAN economies responded to the growth drivers had changed over time. The importance of China had grown substantially, and the magnitude of its impact was the largest since 2010, demonstrating its dominance as a growth driver for the ASEAN6 after the GFC. This outcome looks reasonable, since ASEAN6's trade shares with China had increased in the recent years, reflecting the rise in the trade dependency of these economies with China. For instance, the average cumulative response of ASEAN6 to one-unit expansion in China had increased from 0.51 in 2000 to 1.48 in 2018. The largest impact was observed for Viet Nam, where it increased from 0.33 to 1.61 (5.4 times). On average, the cumulative responses of Indonesia, the Philippines and Thailand jumped by three times, while in Malaysia and Singapore, by two times.

An interesting outcome is the responses of ASEAN6 to shocks from Japan and South Korea. The direct trade links exhibited in Figs. 3.3 and 3.4 revealed that over the sample period, ASEAN6's intermediate exports to Japan were higher than to South Korea. On the contrary, as reported in Table 3.3, the individual ASEAN6's responses to shocks from South Korea were on average, two to three times larger compared to shocks from Japan. This reinforced the presence of South Korea as another major force in the ASEAN6 trade relationship, and the outcome for South Korea can be associated with the impact of the indirect trade channel. In recent times, the influence that each foreign growth driver had on Viet Nam was the largest within the ASEAN6 economies. This indicates that Viet Nam, a fast-growing economy in the region, is more influenced by the foreign growth drivers to help trigger the growth of its economy.

The cumulative average impact of China's shock via the consumption trade channel (as reported in Table 3.4) on ASEAN6 had increased to 0.72 from 0.09 (8 times), confirming further the importance of China as a major force in ASEAN. The multiplier effects of China, South Korea and Japan on Singapore, Thailand and Viet Nam were roughly similar in 2018, and almost three times larger than those of Indonesia and the Philippines. The impacts of South Korean sourced shocks were slightly larger than the Japanese sourced shocks, with the largest impact on Viet Nam, followed by Singapore and Thailand.

Tables 3.5 and 3.6 report the normalized output multipliers. It shows the impact of a one percent positive output growth shock in an economy on the growth of its trading partner in the sample, for the given 2018 weights. It allows us to compare the significance of trading partners in the transmission of shocks between the economies in the sample. These results illustrate the changing nature of international trade patterns across the two categories of trade exports, and the significance of incorporating these changes while examining global interdependencies. The columns indicate the responses of the sample country (12 economies) to a one percent positive output growth shock that originates in the given economies listed in the rows. For instance,

Table 3.5 Normalized output-multipliers, based on 2018 W-matrix of intermediate goods

	IDN	MYS	PHL	SGP	THA	VNM	CHN	JPN	KOR	AU	NZ	IND
IDN	1.00	0.19	0.07	0.18	0.15	0.16	0.14	0.08	0.17	0.01	0.08	−0.12
MYS	0.29	1.00	0.13	0.25	0.18	0.26	0.25	0.18	0.28	0.02	0.09	−0.07
PHL	0.18	0.19	1.00	0.16	0.20	0.17	0.16	0.10	0.19	0.02	0.06	−0.02
SGP	0.35	0.44	0.17	1.00	0.15	0.28	0.28	0.21	0.31	0.04	0.10	−0.05
THA	0.28	0.31	0.15	0.18	1.00	0.28	0.27	0.25	0.30	0.04	0.09	−0.03
VNM	0.24	0.26	0.13	0.19	0.24	1.00	0.24	0.22	0.36	0.04	0.09	−0.01
CHN	0.96	1.09	0.58	0.88	0.94	0.98	1.00	0.91	1.23	0.22	0.52	−0.05
JPN	0.48	0.51	0.35	0.34	0.47	0.45	0.41	1.00	0.51	0.09	0.20	−0.04
KOR	0.34	0.33	0.19	0.21	0.24	0.42	0.37	0.35	1.00	0.07	0.14	0.00
AU	0.14	0.17	0.07	0.11	0.17	0.14	0.15	0.14	0.17	1.00	0.24	0.00
NZ	0.07	0.06	0.02	0.02	0.02	0.08	0.10	0.08	0.10	0.07	1.00	0.00
IND	0.24	0.25	0.10	0.20	0.21	0.19	0.16	0.15	0.22	0.04	0.09	1.00

Notes The columns indicate the responses of the sample country to a 1% positive output growth shock that originates in the given economies listed in the rows. See Table A.1 for country codes
Source Authors' own estimation

Table 3.6 Normalized output-multipliers, based on 2018 W-matrix of Consumption goods

	IDN	MYS	PHL	SGP	THA	VNM	CHN	JPN	KOR	AU	NZ	IND
IDN	1.00	0.13	0.00	0.16	0.08	0.06	0.11	0.06	0.10	0.00	0.04	0.00
MYS	0.13	1.00	0.04	0.18	0.09	0.11	0.21	0.14	0.17	0.00	0.06	−0.01
PHL	0.09	0.11	1.00	0.12	0.10	0.07	0.12	0.06	0.10	0.01	0.04	0.00
SGP	0.21	0.39	0.06	1.00	0.12	0.18	0.31	0.24	0.25	0.04	0.07	0.01
THA	0.15	0.23	0.07	0.23	1.00	0.17	0.27	0.23	0.22	0.04	0.06	0.01
VNM	0.14	0.24	0.08	0.25	0.26	1.00	0.27	0.23	0.29	0.04	0.07	0.02
CHN	0.35	0.52	0.29	0.61	0.56	0.46	1.00	0.65	0.76	0.14	0.36	0.03
JPN	0.32	0.48	0.31	0.51	0.58	0.38	0.56	1.00	0.59	0.10	0.18	0.02
KOR	0.19	0.24	0.15	0.29	0.19	0.29	0.44	0.38	1.00	0.07	0.09	0.02
AU	0.13	0.23	0.07	0.24	0.22	0.13	0.23	0.20	0.20	1.00	0.22	0.02
NZ	0.04	0.06	0.02	0.04	0.03	0.05	0.13	0.08	0.07	0.07	1.00	0.01
IND	0.04	0.08	0.02	0.07	0.06	0.04	0.06	0.05	0.06	0.01	0.02	1.00

Notes The columns indicate the responses of the sample country to a 1% positive output growth shock that originates in the given economies listed in the rows. See Table A.1 for country codes
Source Authors' own estimation

a one percent output shock from China triggered a 0.96% response in Indonesia, while a one percent output shock from Indonesia triggered only a 0.14% response in China. Across the ASEAN6, the impact of a one percent shock in China prompted responses between 0.58% and 1.09%, with Malaysia having incurred the largest impact and the Philippines with the lowest impact. A one percent shock in India only triggered responses between 10% and 25% among the ASEAN6.

The influence of the Chinese output shock was also large in Japan and South Korea, with a response rate of 0.91% and 1.23% respectively. Overall, China's responses to shocks originating from ASEAN6 were less compared to its own influence on these economies. Amongst the economies in the sample, shocks from Japan and South Korea had the largest effect on China, 0.41%, and 0.37% respectively. In addition, there was also a strong interdependence between Japan and South Korea, where Japan's response to South Korea was 0.35%, while South Korea's response to Japan was 0.51%.

Although China still dominates in triggering growth in the region via the consumption goods channel, the average impact was lower compared to the impact coming through the intermediate goods channel (see Table 3.6). The impact of a one percent shock in China prompted responses between 0.29% and 0.61% across the ASEAN6. The responses of the ASEAN6 to a Japanese shock was almost like that of China, prompting that both Japan and China were important growth drivers for shocks penetrating through the consumption goods channel. In turn, China's response to shocks from the region transmitting through the consumption trade channel had similar response to shocks spreading via the intermediate channel.

Zooming in on the intra-ASEAN6 relationships, we observed larger responses of Malaysia and Indonesia to shocks from Singapore and Thailand, while the response of the latter two economies to the former two were considerably lower. Viet Nam also appeared to be a key player in the region, faring much better than Indonesia and the Philippines, with smaller responses to shocks from those economies.

Finally, Tables 3.7 and 3.8 report the output growth co-movements within ASEAN6 for intermediate goods and consumption goods respectively. Both tables illustrate that the output effects of economies within the region were limited. However, economic cooperation and trade agreements among these economies have gradually increased their output growth co-movements, particularly for the linkages between Indonesia and Malaysia with Singapore. It shows that the multiplier effects of ASEAN6 (except Viet Nam) on the output growth of other ASEAN6 economies peaked in 2005 and thereafter the effects started to decline. A similar pattern was observed across the two categories of goods. However, if we compare the recent weights with the 2000 weights, the intra-ASEAN6 growth interdependencies had clearly increased, reflecting their strengthened business cycle synchrony.

3.5.3 Policy Implications

The rapid trade-based growth of China provides both challenges and opportunities to the ASEAN6 economies. China's growth was instrumental in the integration of the dynamic ASEAN region via the intermediate and consumption goods channel. The importance of ASEAN6 economies had rapidly increased in the sample of countries examined, underpinning interest to better understand the region. The economic

Table 3.7 Intra-ASEAN6 output co-movements for intermediate goods

ASEAN6	IDN				MYS				PHL			
	2000	2005	2010	2018	2000	2005	2010	2018	2000	2005	2010	2018
IDN	1.63	1.88	1.68	1.55	0.40	0.54	0.40	0.30	0.08	0.13	0.10	0.07
MYS	0.58	0.76	0.60	0.45	1.86	1.75	1.65	1.54	0.18	0.21	0.15	0.13
PHL	0.27	0.39	0.33	0.28	0.30	0.31	0.32	0.29	1.02	1.04	1.03	1.04
SGP	0.71	0.92	0.73	0.54	1.06	0.90	0.77	0.67	0.21	0.22	0.18	0.18
THA	0.44	0.64	0.52	0.44	0.43	0.53	0.51	0.48	0.10	0.14	0.14	0.15
VNM	0.17	0.28	0.28	0.37	0.16	0.22	0.27	0.40	0.03	0.05	0.07	0.13
ASEAN6	SGP				THA				VNM			
	2000	2005	2010	2018	2000	2005	2010	2018	2000	2005	2010	2018
IDN	0.14	0.37	0.31	0.20	0.38	0.34	0.22	0.15	0.19	0.26	0.21	0.24
MYS	0.44	0.40	0.41	0.28	0.18	0.22	0.20	0.18	0.25	0.30	0.31	0.39
PHL	0.11	0.14	0.23	0.18	0.20	0.25	0.23	0.20	0.13	0.16	0.17	0.25
SGP	1.14	1.15	1.20	1.13	0.22	0.22	0.19	0.15	0.30	0.37	0.34	0.43
THA	0.14	0.20	0.25	0.21	0.97	1.00	0.99	0.99	0.16	0.24	0.27	0.43
VNM	0.03	0.07	0.13	0.21	0.05	0.09	0.14	0.24	1.20	1.24	1.28	1.51

Notes The rows indicate the responses of the individual ASEAN6 economies due to shocks in other members listed in the columns with the given W-matrices of intermediate goods. See Table A.1 for country codes
Source Authors' own estimation

outlook for the ASEAN6 relied on the level of engagement and prospects of major growth drivers, such as China, Japan, and South Korea, and how they affect one another. Of the main driver economies examined, China had the most dominant connections for ASEAN6, followed by South Korea and Japan. The changing trade links were associated with the increasing influence of China—given the fact that the output growth of ASEAN6 was reflected by its trade linkages.

The findings can be explained herein. China's industrialization had restructured ASEAN6 economies towards a regional production chain based on final assembly in China from where the product is exported to other regions. Therefore, China's growth nurtured openness among ASEAN6 economies, and increased trade integration with both China and the rest of the non-ASEAN RCEP economies. As stated by the International Monetary Fund (IMF 2014), the expansion of the Chinese economy provided a cushion for ASEAN economies from other international influences, such as the weakening of the global economy following the GFC. However, China's trade-biased growth also presented challenges for economies with complex trade links within the broader architecture of the RCEP. For some economies, such as Indonesia, Malaysia and Viet Nam, China's progressive growth hindered their trade and manufacturing base due to crowding out (Dungey et al. 2018).

The ASEAN6 advanced their economic interactions with China, mainly in the aftermath of the GFC when the United States (US) became less influential in the

Table 3.8 Intra-ASEAN6 output co-movements for consumption goods

ASEAN6	IDN				MYS				PHL			
	2000	2005	2010	2018	2000	2005	2010	2018	2000	2005	2010	2018
IDN	1.35	1.38	1.37	1.38	0.12	0.19	0.17	0.18	0.01	0.02	0.02	0.00
MYS	0.14	0.16	0.15	0.18	1.33	1.32	1.32	1.34	0.02	0.03	0.05	0.04
PHL	0.04	0.05	0.06	0.12	0.08	0.08	0.09	0.15	0.96	0.96	0.97	0.98
SGP	0.30	0.28	0.27	0.30	0.52	0.51	0.47	0.52	0.04	0.04	0.06	0.06
THA	0.10	0.11	0.15	0.20	0.12	0.18	0.27	0.31	0.02	0.04	0.06	0.07
VNM	0.04	0.04	0.08	0.20	0.07	0.06	0.13	0.32	0.01	0.01	0.04	0.07
ASEAN6	SGP				THA				VNM			
	2000	2005	2010	2018	2000	2005	2010	2018	2000	2005	2010	2018
IDN	0.09	0.27	0.22	0.17	0.09	0.09	0.07	0.07	0.04	0.03	0.03	0.08
MYS	0.23	0.20	0.23	0.20	0.09	0.09	0.07	0.08	0.06	0.05	0.06	0.15
PHL	0.09	0.08	0.08	0.13	0.04	0.05	0.06	0.10	0.03	0.03	0.06	0.10
SGP	1.09	1.08	1.11	1.12	0.17	0.12	0.10	0.11	0.11	0.06	0.10	0.24
THA	0.10	0.12	0.24	0.26	0.92	0.92	0.93	0.96	0.04	0.03	0.07	0.23
VNM	0.08	0.07	0.13	0.29	0.03	0.03	0.08	0.25	1.17	1.17	1.19	1.35

Notes The rows indicate the responses of the individual ASEAN6 economies due to shocks in other members listed in the columns with the given W-matrices of intermediate goods. See Table A.1 for country codes
Source Authors' own estimation

region. However, the continuous economic growth in the wider Asia shifted the economic epicenter towards East Asia, where China, South Korea and Japan emerged as major drivers in the ASEAN region. Nonetheless, Japan's approach to its associations with the ASEAN6 as an investor and trading partner had been somewhat pragmatic.

3.6 Conclusion

This chapter evaluates the role of bilateral trade links *via* intermediate goods, and consumption goods in the international propagation of economic instabilities, using quarterly data on 12 economies (ASEAN6 and non-ASEAN RCEP) for the period 1995 to 2018. We applied the trade-linked VAR framework with time varying weights. The results demonstrated the propagation mechanism between economies through two types of cross-border channels—direct trade links and indirect third market links. The indirect multipliers refer to the cumulative impulse responses after four quarters, while the direct links are via bilateral export shares. The changing trade structure contributed to changes in the responses of ASEAN6 output shocks from China and the non-ASEAN RCEP members. The international propagation patterns had changed substantially. We evaluated the impact of growth shocks from major economies on ASEAN6 and demonstrated the dominance of the China in disseminating shocks in the region.

Our results indicate that growth interdependence among the ASEAN region had increased in 2018 relative to 2000. The results point to hidden vulnerabilities as ASEAN6 are small open economies without the necessary power, to affect the international business cycle with its own growth dynamics. For example, the changes documented in this chapter have had positive, stabilizing effects on ASEAN6's business cycle due to shocks from China. However, when China's growth began to slow down significantly, negative, and destabilizing effects prevailed in the region. The ASEAN6 economies, therefore, need to devise policies regarding their excessive dependence on the external growth drivers, to minimize the adverse effects of economic instabilities to improve their growth prospect. For instance, whilst designing policies to eliminate or minimize the effects of undesirable disturbances, identifying both the origin of shocks and channels via which these shocks propagate are seemingly important.

From the above, the main challenge for ASEAN6 is to offer a competitive environment that will expand their adaptability and productivity relative to China, Japan, and South Korea. ASEAN6 economies can become more competitive and improve their investment opportunities with trade and investment liberalization and facilitation. This chapter contributes to the policy discussion by identifying the significance of trade interdependencies in the propagation of shocks. We showed how the changing trade patterns over time have influenced the propagation mechanism and illustrated the significance of different trade channels in disseminating economic shocks.

References

Abeysinghe, T., & Forbes, K. (2005). Trade linkages and output-multiplier effects: A structural VAR approach with a focus on Asia. *Review of International Economics, 13*(2), 356–375.

Baig, T., & Goldfajn, I. (1999). Financial market contagion in the Asian crisis. *IMF Staff Papers, 46*(2), 167–195.

Baxter, M., & King, R. G. (1999). Measuring business cycles: Approximate band-pass filters for economic time series. *Review of Economics and Statistics, 81*(4), 575–593.

Baxter, M., & Kouparitsas, M. A. (2005). Determinants of business cycle comovement: A robust analysis. *Journal of Monetary Economics, 52*(1), 113–157.

Berkmen, S. P., Gelos, G., Rennhack, R., & Walsh, J. P. (2012). The global financial crisis: Explaining cross-country differences in the output impact. *Journal of International Money and Finance, 31*(1), 42–59.

Blanchard, O. J., Faruqee, H., Das, M., Forbes, K. J., & Tesar, L. L. (2010). The initial impact of the crisis on emerging market countries. *Brookings Papers on Economic Activity, 1,* 263–307.

Burstein, A., Kurz, C., & Tesar, L. (2008). Trade, production sharing, and the international transmission of business cycles. *Journal of Monetary Economics, 55*(4), 775–795.

Calderon, C., Chong, A., & Stein, E. (2007). Trade intensity and business cycle synchronization: Are developing countries any different? *Journal of International Economics, 71*(1), 2–21.

Canova, F. (1991). The sources of financial crisis: Pre- and post-Fed evidence. *International Economic Review, 32*(3), 689–713.

Canova, F., & Dellas, H. (1993). Trade interdependence and the international business cycle. *Journal of International Economics, 34*(1–2), 23–47.
Caselli, F., Koren, M., Lisicky, M., & Tenreyro, S. (2015). Diversification through trade. NBER Working Paper No. 21498, National Bureau of Economic Research (NBER): Washington DC.
Cavallo, E. A., & Frankel, J. A. (2008). Does openness to trade make countries more vulnerable to sudden stops, or less? Using gravity to establish causality. *Journal of International Money and Finance, 27*(8), 1430–1452.
Cesa-Bianchi, A., Pesaran, M.H., Rebucci, A., & Xu, T.T. (2012). China's emergence in the world economy and business cycles in Latin America. *Economía (Brookings Institution Press), 12*(2), 1–75.
Cheewatrakoolpong, K., & Manprasert, S. (2014). Trade linkages and crisis spillovers. *Asian Economic Papers, 13*(1), 84–103.
Cheewatrakoolpong, K., & Manprasert, S. (2015). Trade diversification and crisis transmission: A case study of Thailand. *Asian Economic Journal, 29*(4), 385–408.
Chiang, M. H. (2019). China–ASEAN economic relations after establishment of free trade area. *The Pacific Review, 32*(3), 267–290.
Clark, T. E., & Van Wincoop, E. (2001). Borders and business cycles. *Journal of International Economics, 55*(1), 59–85.
da Costa Neto, N. C., & Romeu, R. (2011). Did export diversification soften the impact of the global financial crisis? IMF Working Paper No. 11/99, International Monetary Fund (IMF): Washington DC.
Dées, S., & Zorell, N. (2012). Business cycle synchronization: Disentangling trade and financial linkages. *Open Economies Review, 23*(4), 623–643.
Di Giovanni, J., & Levchenko, A. A. (2012). Country size, international trade, and aggregate fluctuations in granular economies. *Journal of Political Economy, 120*(6), 1083–1132.
Dungey, M., & Martin, V. L. (1998). Contagion in the East Asian currency crisis. La Trobe University, Mimeo. Retrieved from https://www.business.latrobe.edu.au/staffhp/mardihp/mardi.3.1.
Dungey, M., Vehbi, T., & Martin, C. (2014). VAR modelling in the presence of China's rise: An application to the Taiwanese economy. TSBE Discussion Paper Series N 2014-09, Tasmanian School of Business and Economics: University of Tasmania.
Dungey, M., Khan, F., & Raghavan, M. (2018). International trade and the transmission of shocks: The case of ASEAN-4 and NIE-4 economies. *Economic Modelling, 72,* 109–121.
Edwards, S. (2004). Financial openness, sudden stops, and current-account reversals. *American Economic Review, 94*(2), 59–64.
Feldkircher, M. (2014). The determinants of vulnerability to the global financial crisis 2008 to 2009: Credit growth and other sources of risk. *Journal of International Money and Finance, 43,* 19–49.
Fidrmuc, J., & Korhonen, I. (2010). The impact of the global financial crisis on business cycles in Asian emerging economies. *Journal of Asian Economics, 21*(3), 293–303.
Forbes, K. J. (2004). The Asian flu and Russian virus: The international transmission of crises in firm-level data. *Journal of International Economics, 63*(1), 59–92.
Frankel, J. A., & Rose, A. K. (1998). The endogeneity of the optimum currency area criteria. *The Economic Journal, 108*(449), 1009–1025.
Gruben, W. C., Koo, J., & Millis, E. (2002). How much does international trade affect business cycle synchronization? Research Department Working Paper No. 0203. Federal Reserve Bank of Dallas.
Haidar, J. I. (2012). Currency crisis transmission through international trade. *Economic Modelling, 29*(2), 151–157.
Harrigan, J. (2000). The impact of the Asia crisis on US industry: An almost-free lunch? *Economic Policy Review, 6*(3), 71–81.
Hesse, H. (2008). Export diversification and economic growth. Commission of Growth and Development Working Paper No. 21, World Bank: Washington DC.

Imbs, J. (2004). Trade, finance, specialization, and synchronization. *Review of Economics and Statistics, 86*(3), 723–734.
Ito, T., & Hashimoto, Y. (2005). High-frequency contagion of currency crises in Asia. *Asian Economic Journal, 19*(4), 357–381.
Kali, R., & Reyes, J. (2010). Financial contagion on the international trade network. *Economic Inquiry, 48*(4), 1072–1101.
Kappler, M. (2011). Business cycle co-movement and trade intensity in the Euro Area: Is there a dynamic link? *Journal of Economics and Statistics, 231*(2), 247–265.
Kose, M. A., & Yi, K. M. (2006). Can the standard international business cycle model explain the relation between trade and comovement? *Journal of International Economics, 68*(2), 267–295.
Kuroiwa, I., & Kuwamori, H. (2010). Shock transmission mechanism of the economic crisis in East Asia: An application of international input-output analysis. IDE Discussion Paper No. 220, Institute of Developing Economies (IDE): Japan External Trade Organization (JETRO).
Kurz, C., & Senses, M. Z. (2016). Importing, exporting, and firm-level employment volatility. *Journal of International Economics, 98,* 160–175.
Martin, P., & Rey, H. (2006). Globalization and emerging markets: With or without crash? *American Economic Review, 96*(5), 1631–1651.
Masson, P. (1999). Contagion: Monsoonal effects, spillovers and jumps between multiple equilibria. In P. R. Agenor, M. Miller, D. Vines, & A. Weber (Eds.), *The Asian financial crisis: Causes, contagion and consequences* (pp.265–280). Cambridge, United Kingdom: Cambridge University Press.
Otto, G., Voss, G., & Willard, L. (2001). Understanding OECD output correlations. RBA Discussion Papers 2001–05, Reserve Bank of Australia.
Pentecôte, J. S., & Rondeau, F. (2015). Trade spillovers on output growth during the 2008 financial crisis. *International Economics, 143,* 36–47.
Perry, G., & Lederman, D. (1998). *Financial vulnerability, spillover effects and contagion: Lessons from the Asian Crises for Latin America.* Washington, DC: World Bank.
Rose, A. K., & Spiegel, M. M. (2011). Cross-country causes and consequences of the crisis: An update. *European Economic Review, 55*(3), 309–324.
Sato, K., & Shrestha, N. (2012). Global and regional shock transmission—New evidence from globally integrated input–output table. Paper presented at the 13th International Convention of the East Asian Economic Association, October 2012, Singapore.
Sato, K., & Shrestha, N. (2014). Global and regional shock transmission—An Asian perspective. CESSA Working Paper No. 2014-04, Centre for Economic and Social Studies in Asia: Yokohama National University.
Shin, K., & Wang, Y. (2005). The impact of trade integration on business cycle co-movements in Europe. *Review of World Economics, 141*(1), 104–123.
Tan, K. Y., Abeysinghe, T., & Tan, K. G. (2015). Shifting drivers of growth: Policy implications for ASEAN-5. *Asian Economic Papers, 14*(1), 157–173.
Tobin, M., & Power, J. (2019). The spoils of trade war: Asia's winners and losers in US–China clash. South China Morning Post. Retrieved from https://www.scmp.com/week-asia/geopolitics/article/3010733/spoils-trade-war-asias-winners-and-losers-us-china-clash.
Yuning, G., & Junyi, Z. (2016). Emerging China and its interaction with ASEAN economies. In Y-C. Kim (Ed.), Chinese global production networks in ASEAN (pp. 1–18). Switzerland: Springer.
Zervoyianni, A., & Anastasiou, A. (2009). Convergence of shocks and trade in the enlarged European Union. *Journal of International Trade & Economic Development, 18*(1), 79–114.

Online Databases

CEIC Database. (2020). Retrieved from https://www.ceicdata.com/en.
IMF. (2020). Direction of trade statistics (DOTS). Retrieved from https://data.imf.org/?sk=9D6028D4-F14A-464C-A2F2-59B2CD424B85.
UN Comtrade. (2020). Retrieved from https://comtrade.un.org/data/.
UNCTAD-TRAINS Database. (2021). Retrieved from: https://trains.unctad.org/Default.aspx.
World Bank. (2020). World development indicators. Retrieved from https://databank.worldbank.org/source/world-development-indicators.

Chapter 4
Vulnerability of the Food Sector

4.1 Introduction

Modern food production involves extensive supply chains and multiple inputs, resulting in increasing trade linkages. Increasing trade linkages, in turn, lead to co-movements and increased volatility as they induce large demand-side and supply-side effects. For example, episodes like the US–China trade war (Tobin and Power 2019) and the COVID-19 pandemic have caused a realignment of global supply chains. In the case of COVID-19, partial lockdowns and production stoppages have constrained capacity and exports. The consequence of that is reductions in global supply of food, putting further pressure on food security. Further, disruptions to the supply chain are evident from the pandemic, as some countries resort to abandoning liberal trade policies in favour of domestic protection to mitigate the effects of short-run food crises. For example, regional producers like Thailand, Cambodia, and Viet Nam, had resorted to export bans or moratorium on new export contracts for staple foods. The introduction of new export restrictions by regional and global food producers in response to the pandemic further limited global supply and restricted market access.

Supply chain disruptions and trade restrictions are thereby putting pressure on national and regional food availability. The US–China trade war and the Covid-19 pandemic, as in any other short- to medium-term trade (output) shocks, is considered a hiatus during which the food security worsens. It is therefore important to understand the linkages between trade and food security to enhance trade resilience and improve the status of food security, particularly in the ASEAN region. International trade reduces food insecurity by connecting countries with limited agriculture potential and providing access to diversified food for the importers. Trade also plays a balancing role by evening out demand and supply fluctuations. Food availability is therefore determined by international trade patterns, and to some extent, food security at the regional level rests on trade (Farsund et al. 2015).

China, given its sheer size and regional presence, through food demand, supply, and trade (Fold et al. 2011), is a crucial player in the regional and global markets for food products (intermediate and final goods). This chapter therefore examines

M. Raghavan et al., *China and ASEAN: Pivoting Trade and Shock Transmission*,
https://doi.org/10.1007/978-981-16-1618-1_4

the relative importance of trade links with China in transmitting economic shocks from the context of food trade, since the shocks are reported to be absorbed disproportionately across the low to medium and high-income countries (Distefano et al. 2018). Importantly, the expected enhancement of trade linkage raises the importance of examining the role of global food import sources and export destinations in transmitting trade shocks to the AMS, directly and indirectly through other parties in the region. The propagation of food trade shocks to the AMS may also prove to be somewhat different from aggregate export shocks given their varying food trade dynamics and interdependencies with China and the region.

As there are many indicators to capture the multifaceted concept of food security, this chapter focuses on the dimension of availability[22] (access) based on indicators of trade and trade policy. They are: First, the ASEAN region's reliance on agro-food (hereafter referred to as food), namely the trade dependence; and Second, ASEAN's export exposure and export resilience to regional and global trade shocks in food. The export resiliency is important as it captures the potentials for increasing food exports, which in turn are important for financing imports. The assessment of the extent of interdependencies and effects of food trade shocks, and the related intersection of trade policy, are essential for guiding the region to better manage its vulnerability to trade shocks and develop better capacity for evaluating policy tradeoffs (see also Smith and Glauber 2019).

This chapter begins with an examination of China's food trade data to document how patterns of trade are changing with the ASEAN region. Then follows a comparison of the food trade regulations in China and ASEAN in Sect. 4.3. Section 4.4 describes the data and changes in output growth and export shares. Section 4.5 presents the empirical results based on the cumulative impulse responses of ASEAN6 to output shocks and the output multipliers. Section 4.6 concludes.

4.2 China–ASEAN: Food Trade Flows

ASEAN represented 14.54% of China's total trade in food (including beverages) in 1998, and the regional market share increased marginally to 17.67% in 2019. China's exports of food to ASEAN grew at an annual average of 14.30% relative to 15.34% of food imports from the region for 1998 to 2019. Though China is acknowledged globally as a net food exporter (van Tongeren and Huang 2004), China is net importer of food from the region, as shown in Fig. 4.1. It's major export markets in the region are Viet Nam, followed by Thailand, Malaysia, the Philippines, and Indonesia. From the perspective of imports, the major regional sources are Thailand, followed by Indonesia, Viet Nam, and Malaysia. These major markets accounted for 90.93% and 88.49% of China's total exports to and total imports from ASEAN in 2019, respectively. The big areas of growth in China's food import basket are in sectors such as livestock, grains and high-quality, processed foods and beverages, while vegetable, fish, and most livestock commodities have become the major exportable products from China to Southeast Asia (Fold et al. 2011).

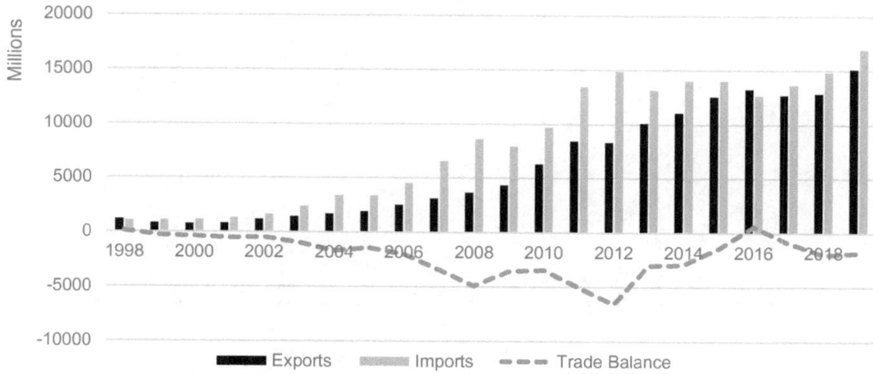

Fig. 4.1 China–ASEAN—Exports, imports and trade balance in food, 1998–2019 (USD million). *Notes* Includes beverages. Based on the BEC codes (111, 112, 121 and 122; See Table A.2). *Source* UN Comtrade (2020)

By broad classifications of food trade, China's exports of food to ASEAN comprised mainly of consumption goods, as shown in Fig. 4.2. While the export patterns have remained the same over the period of review, the import trends of food imports have somewhat changed. Approximately 69.33% of food imports in 1998 were intermediate goods but in 2019, 63.38% of total imports to China comprised consumption goods. The shift in the composition of food imports was from intermediate to consumption (final) goods. The rising imports of food consumption goods are sparked by rising incomes and changing tastes of the Chinese population, and China's own food safety scandals. Fold et al. (2011) adds that China's growth has stimulated considerable change in food consumption patterns and dietary habits, especially within the rapidly growing urban middle-class population, and these trends had potentially provided huge opportunities for high-value food exporters from ASEAN. For example, the variety of food imports from Thailand grew from 61 to 292 between 1992 and 2015 (Sun 2019). Worth mentioning here is that Thailand is also the strongest advocate for China–ASEAN agri-food liberalization under the EHP (see Table 2.1).

Yet Thailand, apart from Indonesia and Malaysia are still more food import dependent on China relative to the other AMS (see Fig. 4.3). Overall, the region has become growingly more dependent on China for trade in food for the 2000 to 2019 period. China, however, is still more important as an export destination relative to an import source for food. China represented 5.18% (6.81%) of the region's total exports (imports) of food in 2000, and 16.36% (10.61%) in 2019. The newer AMS (Myanmar, Cambodia, Lao and Viet Nam) are more food export dependent on China relative to the older AMS. Interestingly, Viet Nam, which was initially sidelined in the food trade business between ASEAN and China, has subsequently gained ground and replaced Thailand in the food export relationship with China.

Even though China runs a deficit in food trade with ASEAN, some perceive that China is a threat to the ASEAN food economy (Fold et al. 2011). China is deemed to

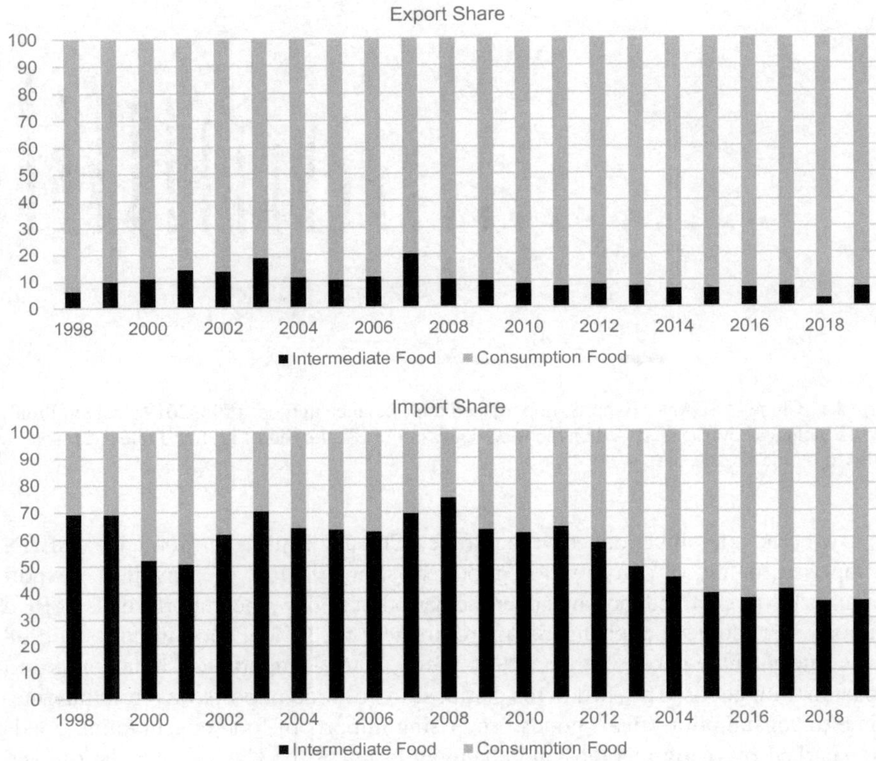

Fig. 4.2 China–ASEAN—Shares of food exports and imports, intermediate and consumption goods, 1998–2019 (%). *Notes* Includes beverages. Based on the BEC codes: 111 & 121 (intermediate goods) and 112 & 122 (consumption goods) for food (See Table A.2). *Source* UN Comtrade (2020)

be reorganizing the world food system given its diverse range of food products that have penetrated the ASEAN and global markets. From the import standpoint, Gale and Huang (2007) argue that studies of food demand in China have in fact overstated its pulling power on world food markets. Recent data indicate that spending on food in China declined from 50% of total household consumption in 2000 to 25% in 2017, like that of urban consumers in developed countries (McKinsey Global Institute 2019). Worth mentioning here is that China is also not considered a natural supporter of agri-food trade liberalization.

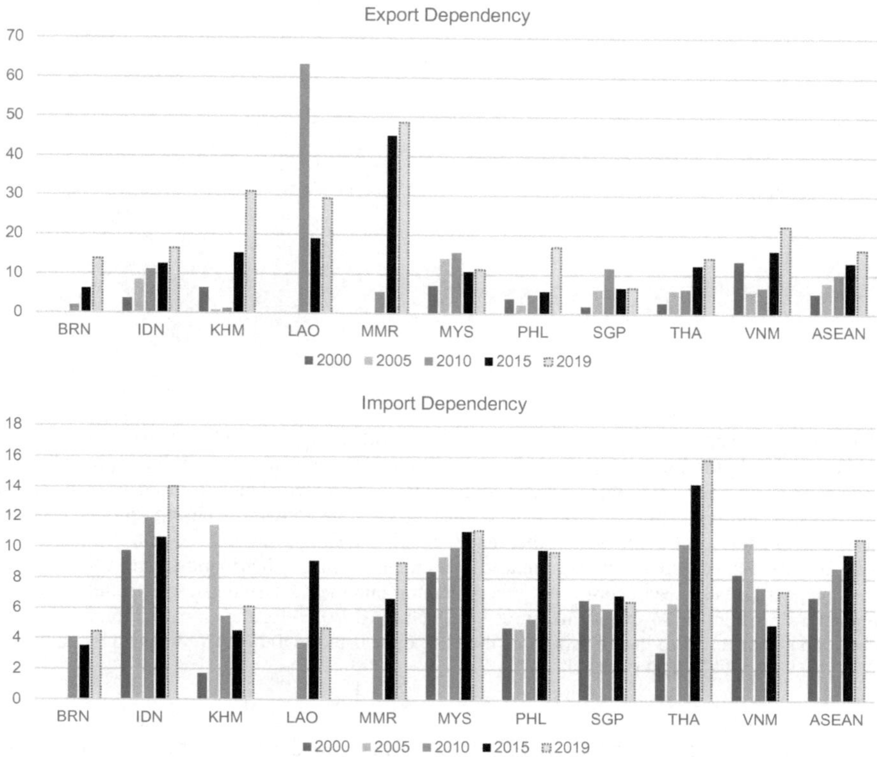

Fig. 4.3 ASEAN—Food trade dependency* on China (%). *Notes* Includes beverages. Based on the BEC codes: 111& 121 (intermediate goods) and 112 & 122 (consumption goods) for food (See Table A.2). *Dependency is calculated as the share of exports (imports) of each AMS to China in its own total exports (imports) of food to the rest of the world. *Source* UN Comtrade (2020)

4.3 China–ASEAN: Food Trade Regulations

Non-tariff measures (NTMs) are identified as a challenge for food trade in ASEAN (Devadason et al. 2018). In terms of the ASEAN's regulatory framework, a total of 5,213 NTMs, constituting 54.98% of public NTMs, are found in food regulations.[23] The incidence of food regulations varies within ASEAN, ranging from a low 27.31% in Lao PDR to a high 72.6% in Brunei. Notwithstanding that, the incidence or food regulations in each of the ASEAN6 member states, with the exception for Indonesia and Viet Nam, exceeds 50% of their total NTMs. Thailand, followed by the Philippines and Malaysia are the most highly regulated markets for food trade in ASEAN. The intensity found in food regulations in China relative to ASEAN is somewhat less at 37.55% of its public NTMs.

At 73.97% and 76.84%, the NTMs are mostly that of technical measures[24] in ASEAN and China respectively (see Fig. 4.4). Of these, 64.47% (70.71%) relate

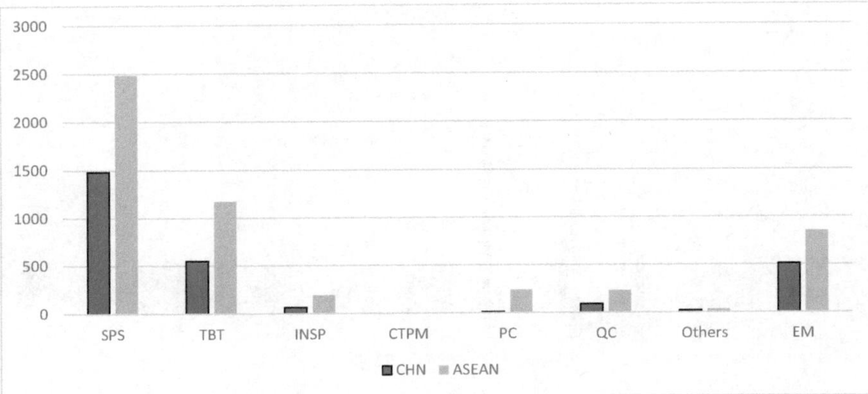

Fig. 4.4 China and ASEAN—Number of NTMs in food sector, by NTM chapters. *Notes*: SPS—sanitary and phytosanitary measures; TBT—technical barriers to trade; INSP—pre-shipment inspection and other formalities; CTPM—contingent trade protective measures; PC—price control measures, including additional taxes and charges; QC—nonautomatic licensing, quotas, prohibitions, and quantity control measures other than for SPS or TBT reasons; Others—finance measures, measures affecting competition, trade-related investment measures, distribution restrictions, restrictions on post-sales services, subsidies, government procurement restrictions, intellectual property, and rules of origin; EM—export measures (see UNCTAD 2015, for the classification of NTMs). The food sector refers to the 18 groups of the HS2-digit listed in Table A.7. *Source* Derived from UNCTAD-TRAINS (2021)

to sanitary and phytosanitary (SPS)[25] measures and 30.47% (26.23%) constitute technical barriers to trade (TBTs) in ASEAN (China). More important than the incidence of NTMs in food in China and ASEAN is the regulatory distance (RD) or proximity in regulation between the former and the latter, as the latter matters for trade costs, and RDs slow down trade considerably (Ing et al. 2019; Nabeshima and Obashi 2019; Cadot and Ing 2015; Cadot et al. 2015). The general idea is that if the regulation for food is the same between China and the AMS, this is not regarded as a barrier to trade. If they differ, then food trade is impeded in one direction but not the other. In short, a more heavily regulated country, should find it easier to export to a less regulated country, than the other way around.

Figure 4.5 reports the RD[26] in technical measures for agriculture (see Table A.7 for 24 products at the HS2-digit level, including food and beverages) trade between China and ASEAN. The RD between China and each AMS in agriculture is high (RD > 0.5) for TBTs relative to SPS and INSP. For comparison, the bilateral RD between China and the AMS are compared with the intra-ASEAN RDs for technical measures in Table A.8. The intra-ASEAN RDs of technical measures for agriculture are generally low ($RD \leq 0.4$). This concurs with the overall findings of Nabeshima and Obashi (2019) in that the implementation patterns of NTMs in ASEAN, unlike the case for China, correlate to the world average pattern. They however qualify that the regulatory dissimilarity varies greatly amongst ASEAN and China, ranging from 0.19 for the Lao PDR to 0.97 for China for non-technical measures, mainly that

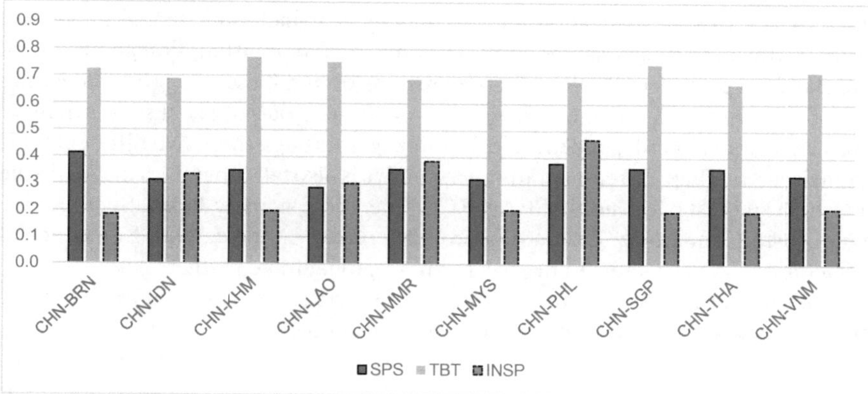

Fig. 4.5 China and ASEAN—Regulatory distance of technical measures in agriculture. *Notes* The RDs measured by construction is symmetric (see endnote 21). A higher value of RD (a value closer to one) indicates a higher regulatory dissimilarity between two countries. SPS—sanitary and phytosanitary measures; TBTs—technical barriers to trade; INSP—pre-shipment inspection and other formalities. *Source* Calculated from UNCTAD-TRAINS (2021)

of Chapters E (non-automatic licensing, quotas, prohibitions, and quantity control measures other than SPS or TBT) and F (price control measures, including additional taxes and charges).

Since technical measures are dominant in food in both China and ASEAN, and the bilateral RD of these measures between China and ASEAN are also found to be high, the intensity and the diversity of NTMs between the former and the latter in food could potentially pose barriers to food trade through market access. Further, the larger dissimilarity in the RD of the dominant NTMs between China and ASEAN relative to intra-ASEAN suggests different implications for food trade following from output shocks. The data analysis on the regulatory framework justifies the case of examining food trade shocks in the region as trade policies may intersect with trade flows to understand the trade resilience (vulnerability) of the AMS.

4.4 Changing Food Trade Patterns

This section details the data on food trade patterns between ASEAN6, China and the other non-ASEAN RCEP members. It mainly provides a quick analysis of the core patterns related to export shares of two broad categories of food—intermediate food and final (also referred to as consumption) food. As in Chap. 3, the bilateral export shares of these two categories of food are measured and their changing patterns are assessed across various times.

The annual intermediate food exports data, and final food exports data, reported in current US dollars, are sourced from the BEC of the UN Comtrade (2020) database.

Based on the BEC classification, intermediate goods (including capital goods) are for industrial and primary sector purposes, while final or consumption goods are for household purposes (see Table A.2). We are considering these two broad categories of food exports, to assess the transmission of China's output shocks on ASEAN6 based on its trade interdependence, and its linkages through these two different trade channels. As in Chap. 3, a comparative perspective is also taken between the ASEAN6 and China and rest of the non-ASEAN RCEP members, namely Japan, South Korea, India, Australia and New Zealand, to provide context on the extent of influence of China on ASEAN6 relative to the other extra-regional trade partners.

As discussed in Chap. 3, to measure bilateral trade flows of food exports, we construct export shares for each economy in our sample.

$$w_{ijt} = \frac{x_{ijt}}{x_{it}} \tag{4.1}$$

where the weights are the exports (x_{ijt}) from country i to country j respectively divided by total exports (x_{it}) of country i at time t.

The export-weighted series for each economy is constructed as follows:

$$\sum_{j=1}^{n} w_{ijt} = w_{i1t} + w_{i2t} + \cdots + w_{int} = 1 \quad \text{where } i \neq j \tag{4.2}$$

where $i \neq j$; $j = 1, 2, \ldots, n$.

To reduce the noise in the series, the export weighted series is smoothed using the three-year moving average method.

Table 4.1 reports the regional export share for regional export shares for intermediate food and final food of the ASEAN6 economies, respectively. In 2018, around 50% of ASEAN6's intermediate food exports were to the 12 economies in the sample, if we decompose this further, 19% of the exports were destined to the ASEAN6, while 8% to China, and 23% were to the other non-ASEAN RCEP (excluding China) countries. Amongst the ASEAN6, Singapore and Thailand commanded the highest export shares of intermediate food to the 12 countries in 2018, at approximately 64% and 68% respectively, while the Philippines recorded the lowest export share at 14%. Unlike the case of total intermediate goods reported in Chap. 3, ASEAN6's intermediate food exports to China had remained stable over the sample period, hovering between 6% and 8%. In terms of intra-regional trade, at 46%, Thailand garnered the largest share of intermediate food exports to ASEAN6 in 2018. Except for Thailand, the average intra-regional trade in intermediate food of ASEAN6 did not vary much for the past 18 years. Interestingly, Viet Nam's intermediate food exports to the region shrunk sharply from 21% in 2000 to only 8% in 2018.

As reported in the bottom panel of Table 4.1, in 2018, around 54% of ASEAN6's exports of final food were to the country sample. Notably, the bilateral export share of final food of Viet Nam to China was three times larger than the export share of intermediate food for that same year. In terms of intra-regional (or intra-ASEAN6)

Table 4.1 ASEAN6 - regional export shares of food

ASEAN6	Exports to country sample[a]			Exports to ASEAN6			Exports to China		
	2000	2010	2018	2000	2010	2018	2000	2010	2018
Intermediate food exports									
Indonesia	0.42	0.56	0.46	0.17	0.16	0.11	0.05	0.13	0.13
Malaysia	0.49	0.43	0.43	0.12	0.09	0.15	0.10	0.23	0.11
Philippines	0.15	0.16	0.14	0.06	0.05	0.05	0.02	0.03	0.03
Singapore	0.54	0.54	0.64	0.26	0.20	0.29	0.03	0.04	0.11
Thailand	0.63	0.66	0.68	0.29	0.39	0.46	0.05	0.05	0.05
Viet Nam	0.39	0.21	0.26	0.21	0.08	0.08	0.09	0.04	0.06
Average	0.44	0.46	0.50	0.19	0.16	0.19	0.06	0.08	0.08
Final food exports									
Indonesia	0.57	0.42	0.49	0.16	0.18	0.27	0.04	0.04	0.10
Malaysia	0.59	0.64	0.67	0.43	0.48	0.47	0.02	0.03	0.08
Philippines	0.52	0.45	0.47	0.07	0.16	0.07	0.03	0.02	0.11
Singapore	0.58	0.69	0.71	0.27	0.37	0.43	0.01	0.13	0.06
Thailand	0.24	0.28	0.42	0.08	0.09	0.13	0.03	0.05	0.11
Viet Nam	0.36	0.40	0.47	0.15	0.18	0.10	0.05	0.07	0.22
Average	0.47	0.48	0.54	0.19	0.24	0.25	0.03	0.06	0.11

Note [a] Refers to remaining countries of ASEAN6 and non-ASEAN RCEP
Source Compiled from UNCTADstat (2020)

trade, Malaysia, followed by Singapore occupied the top positions with final food export shares of 47% and 43% respectively. From the export shares, we can conclude that the 12 countries displayed somewhat similar integration patterns for the two groups of food items.

Figure 4.6 further depicts some major changes in the export-shares of intermediate food and final food for China and the ASEAN6 economies with the non-ASEAN RCEP countries for the period 1995Q1 to 2018Q4. Explicitly, it illustrates how the export intensities of the ASEAN6, and China, had evolved over time between the two food export categories. The ASEAN6 economies' direct exports of intermediate food to China, Japan and India were found to be rising, relatively more compared with the other non-ASEAN RCEP trading partners. Interestingly, India's link with the ASEAN6 via the intermediate food export channel was much more important compared to the same link with South Korea. The intermediate food export shares of ASEAN6 to China increased from 3% in 1995 to 15% in 2018, and since 2011, export shares to China were even greater than that to Japan. Intermediate food export shares of ASEAN6 to India were rising from a share of less than one percent in 1995 to 6% in 2018.

Similar as that reported in Chap. 3, Japan has been the leading export destination for ASEAN6's final food based on the right panel of Fig. 4.6. Despite that, the final

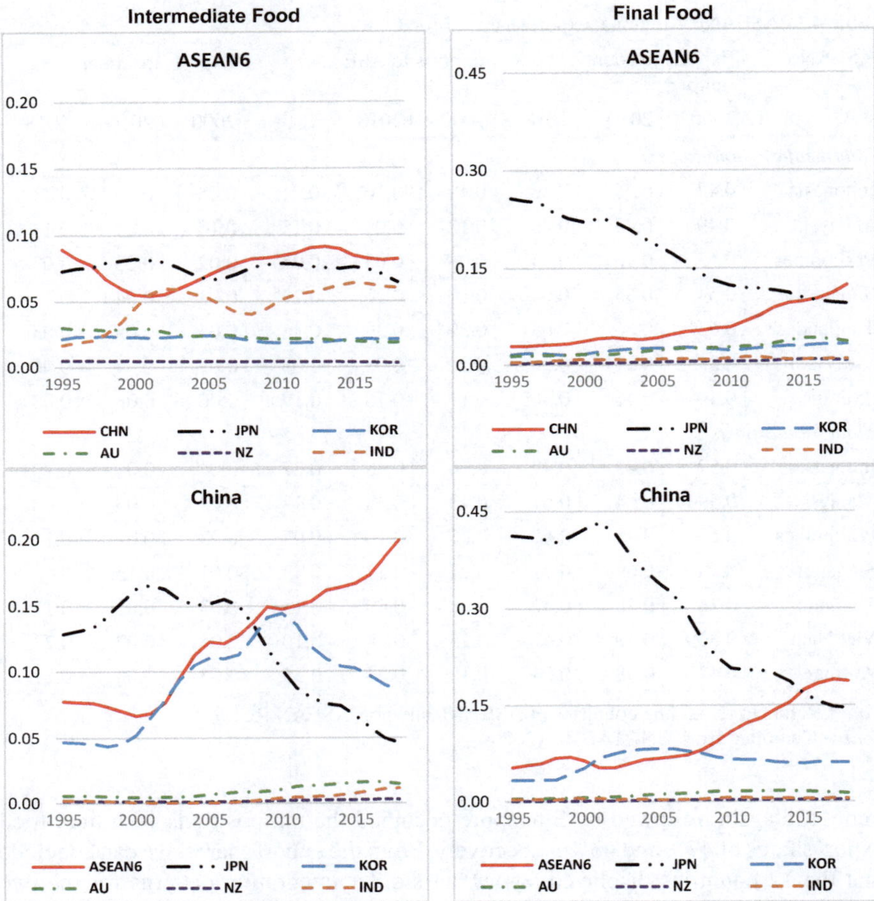

Fig. 4.6 ASEAN6-China—Export shares in intermediate food and final food, 1995–2018. *Note* The vertical axis, export shares of intermediate food and final food, indicate changes in trade patterns of China and ASEAN6. See Table A.1 for country codes. *Source* Author's own compilation

food export shares of ASEAN6 to Japan appears to be on a downward spiral, shifting from 25% in 1995 to 0.9% in 2018. On the other hand, final food export shares of ASEAN6 to China is on an upward trend, rising from 0.3% in 1995 to 12% in 2018. Overall, the ASEAN6's main food export destinations were China and Japan, while India had gained ground as an export destination for intermediate food.

As for China's food exports, a similar pattern emerged as that reported in Chap. 3. Since 2005, the ASEAN6 economies were the main export destinations for China's intermediate food exports compared to its final food exports (see bottom panel of Fig. 4.6). China's exports of intermediate food to ASEAN6 increased from 8% in 1995 to 20% in 2018, and those to Japan declined from 13% to 5% over the same period. In 1995, around 41% of China's final food exports were to Japan, while only 5% was to ASEAN6. However, in 2018, China's final food exports to ASEAN6 (19%) had surpassed that to Japan (13%). This shows, the bilateral trade integration between China and ASEAN6 was growing gradually over time through both food exports channel. Fold et al. (2011) point out that China has a huge capacity to produce massive volumes of differentiated food products at low costs, and subsequently, this has increased food import dependency across Southeast Asia (see also Fig. 4.3).

Figure 4.7 presents the export-shares of intermediate food and final food of the individual ASEAN6 economies to the non-ASEAN RCEP members. Overall, the main exporters of intermediate food were Indonesia, Malaysia and Thailand, and the main export destinations were Japan, China, and India. Viet Nam and the Philippines reported the smallest export shares of intermediate food. If we focus on each ASEAN6's export shares to China, the shares of intermediate food from Indonesia, Malaysia, the Philippines, and Singapore to China had increased, while it decreased from Thailand and Viet Nam. Likewise, intermediate food export shares of Indonesia and Malaysia to India grew over the sample period, while Japan remained the main destination for intermediate food exports from the Philippines, Singapore, and Thailand.

As for final food exports (right panel of Fig. 4.7), Japan was still the major destination for ASEAN6. The final food exports to Japan are varied and the largest suppliers are Thailand and Indonesia, according to Dy (2015). Although Japan is still the major player in the region, the importance of its market for final food exports of each ASEAN6 had sharply declined. Notably, the economic interdependence via the final food channel between Viet Nam and China had increased significantly since 2010. Among the ASEAN6, Malaysia's final food export shares to the non-ASEAN RCEP members remained comparatively the lowest.

Figure 4.8 presents the intra-ASEAN6 links and the connections between the ASEAN6 and China. The patterns of ASEAN6's intermediate food export shares tend to be a mixed bag, indicating that these economies are not overly food dependent on the regional economy. This also indirectly reflects the diverse capacity of ASEAN to produce and export food (Chandra and Lontoh 2010). While Thailand was the main intermediate food exporter to ASEAN, Malaysia was the main intermediate food importer from the region. Overall, since 2005, the export shares of Indonesia, the Philippines and Thailand of intermediate food to China were larger than the export shares to other ASEAN6 members. This is not surprising since Thailand can be considered the first, within ASEAN, to embrace stronger food trade relations with China, having met the EHP implementation timetable (see Table 2.1). Thailand gained easy access to the Chinese market for its exports of fresh fruits and vegetables after the harmonization of food standards between both countries in 2005. A different pattern emerged from the intra-ASEAN6 export shares of final food (see the right panel of Fig. 4.8). Singapore was the largest export destination for final food exports from Malaysia and Indonesia, though the exports from Malaysia were three times larger than that from Indonesia. Viet Nam's final food export shares to China were many folds larger compared to its intra-regional export shares.

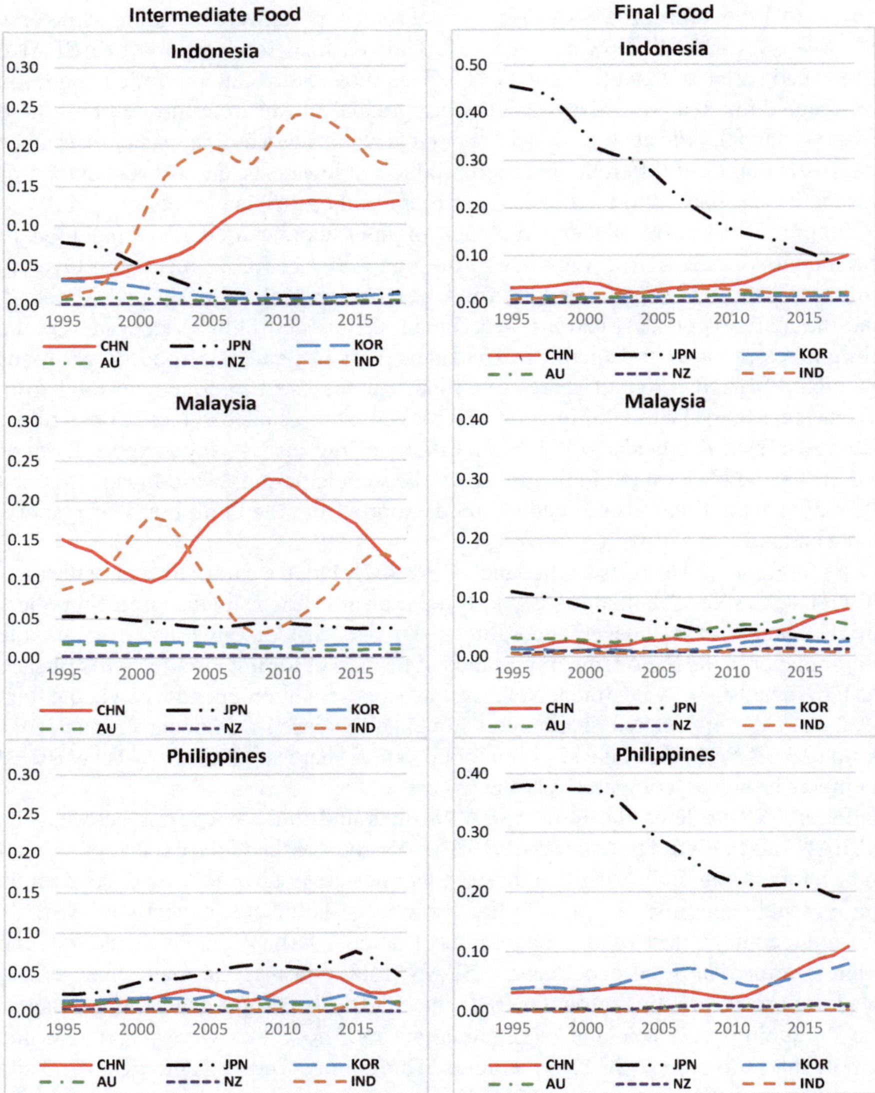

Fig. 4.7 ASEAN6—Export shares in intermediate food and final food to non-ASEAN RCEP, 1995–2018. *Notes* The vertical axis, the export shares of intermediate food and final food, indicate changes in export patterns of the individual ASEAN6 countries with the non-ASEAN RCEP members. See Table A.1 for country codes. *Source* Authors' own compilation

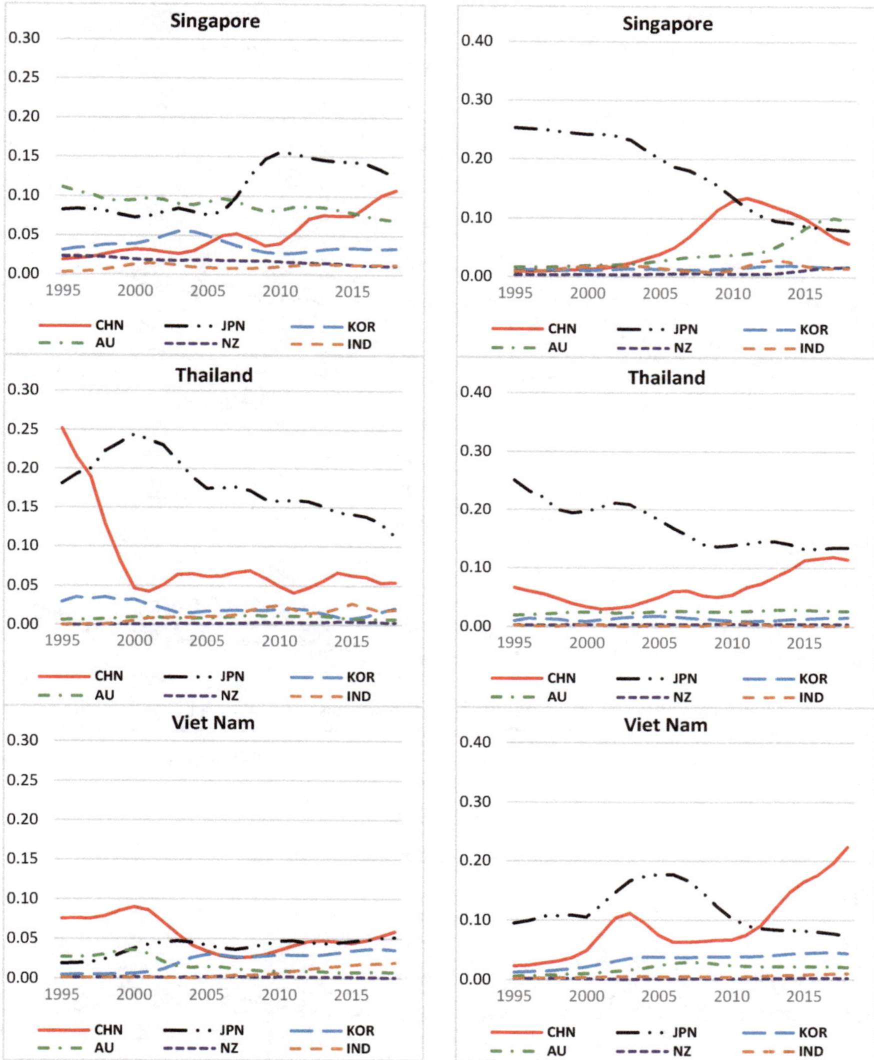

Fig. 4.7 (continued)

The trends observed from Figs. 4.6, 4.7 and 4.8, overall, support the arguments that food trade is relevant to the China–ASEAN engagement, though not as significant as the overall intermediate goods and consumption goods channels (see Chap. 3). Notwithstanding that, the trends in the food export shares suggest a disproportionate influence on ASEAN6 following from output shocks in the regional and extra-regional trading partners.

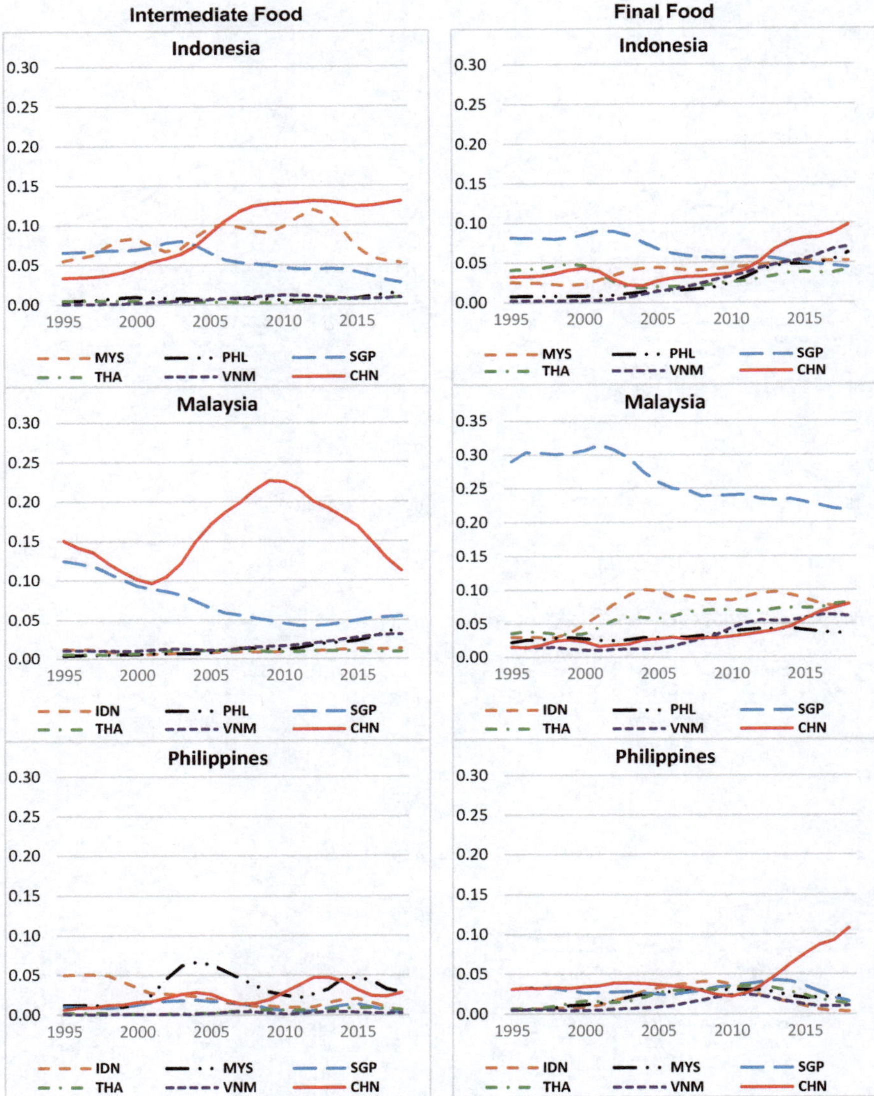

Fig. 4.8 ASEAN6—Export shares in intermediate food and final food to China and ASEAN6, 1995–2018. *Notes* The vertical axis, the export shares of intermediate food and final food, indicate changes in export patterns of the individual ASEAN6 countries with the other ASEAN partners, including China. See Table A.1 for the country codes. *Source* Authors' own compilation

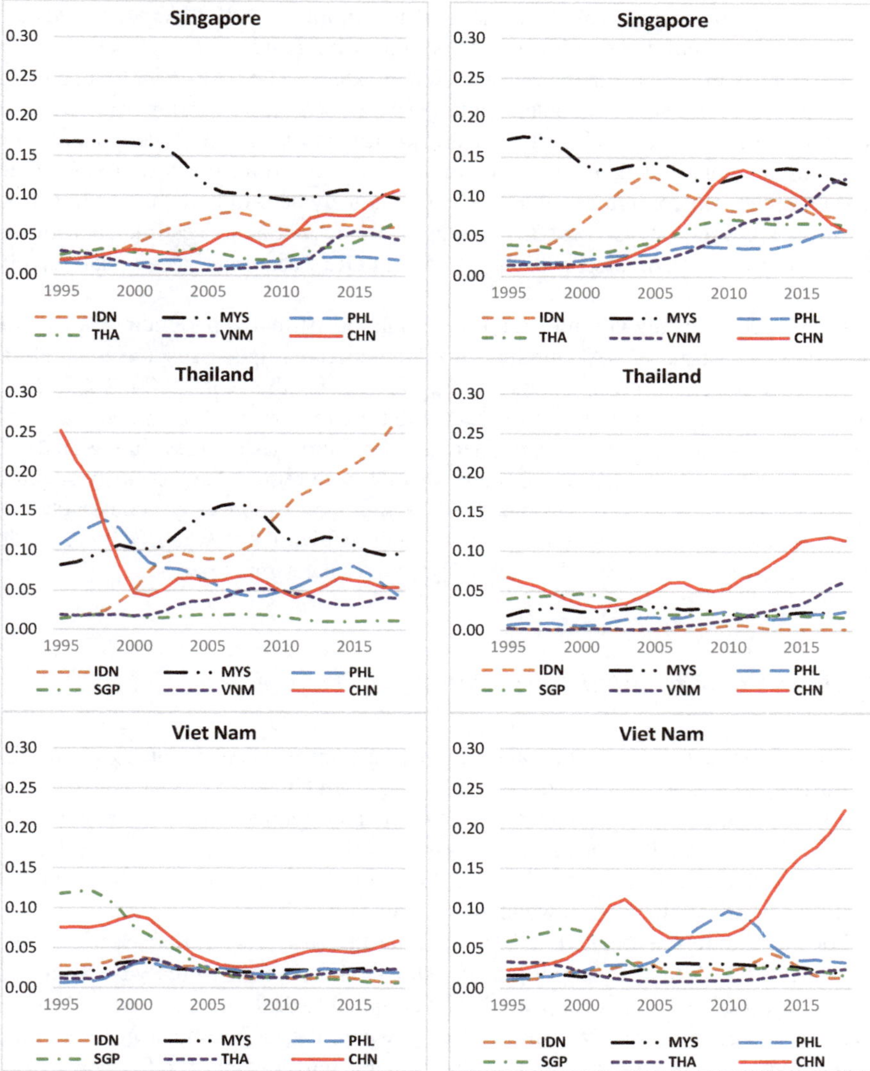

Fig. 4.8 (continued)

4.5 Empirical Results

This section presents the impulse responses for the ASEAN6 economies to the output shocks penetrating through the food trade channels. The output multipliers are reported and discussed to demonstrate the dynamic nature of the transmission mechanism and illustrate the international effects of a country-specific shock over time. Finally, the output growth co-movements within the ASEAN6 economies are explained along with the significance of both the direct and indirect effects.

To quantify the change in the transmission of external shocks to ASEAN6, a set of simulation exercises are conducted using the VAR, with time varying trade weights described in Chap. 3. In the first stage, using the time-varying export weights, foreign variables are constructed, and the VAR model is estimated for the period 1995Q1 to 2018Q4. Since the foreign variables are endogenously determined, the 2SLS is used to estimate the model. As a robustness check, the model is also estimated with the OLS. The results, estimated with the 2SLS and OLS, are found to be qualitatively similar.

In the second stage, with the assumption that the estimated parameters are stable over time, the estimated VAR model is used to generate impulse responses for alternative trade matrices. As in Chap. 3, trade weights for the years 2000, 2005, 2010 and 2018 are employed, and then the resulting time responses of the transmission of specific output shocks are compared across different trade linkages. In the analysis of the international transmission of these shocks, both regional and country-specific responses are considered in this chapter. The regional responses are constructed as weighted averages of the country specific responses. Unlike in Chap. 3, here, we do not identify any marked shift in trade weights over the sample period.

4.5.1 ASEAN6 Impulse Responses

Figure 4.9 presents the accumulated impulse responses of ASEAN6 as group, for 20 quarters due to a one-unit shock originating from China and other non-ASEAN RCEP economies for the different weights of intermediate food (left panel), and final food (right panel) respectively. We assessed the responses for the four different weight matrices—2000, 2005, 2010 and 2018—and the figures clearly showed that impulse responses changed as we altered the weights.

For the models estimated using the intermediate food export weights, the responses of ASEAN6 as a group to the shocks from South Korea were found to be the largest. This outcome appeared to be completely different from using the total intermediate goods export weight (Chap. 3), where the China shock generated the largest impact on ASEAN6. Though the bilateral intermediate food export shares of ASEAN6 to South Korea were not large (refer to Fig. 4.6) compared to China, Japan and India, the effects of a shock from South Korea were unexpectedly much larger compared to these economies. Overall, South Korea's influence on intermediate food in the region was experienced largely through the indirect channel rather than through direct channel. However, with more recent trade weights, that is for trade weights based on 2018, a China output shock mattered much more for intermediate food exports from ASEAN6. With 2018 weights, the effects of intermediate exports to Japan, in turn, became less pronounced despite its strong bilateral food trade relationship with the ASEAN6.

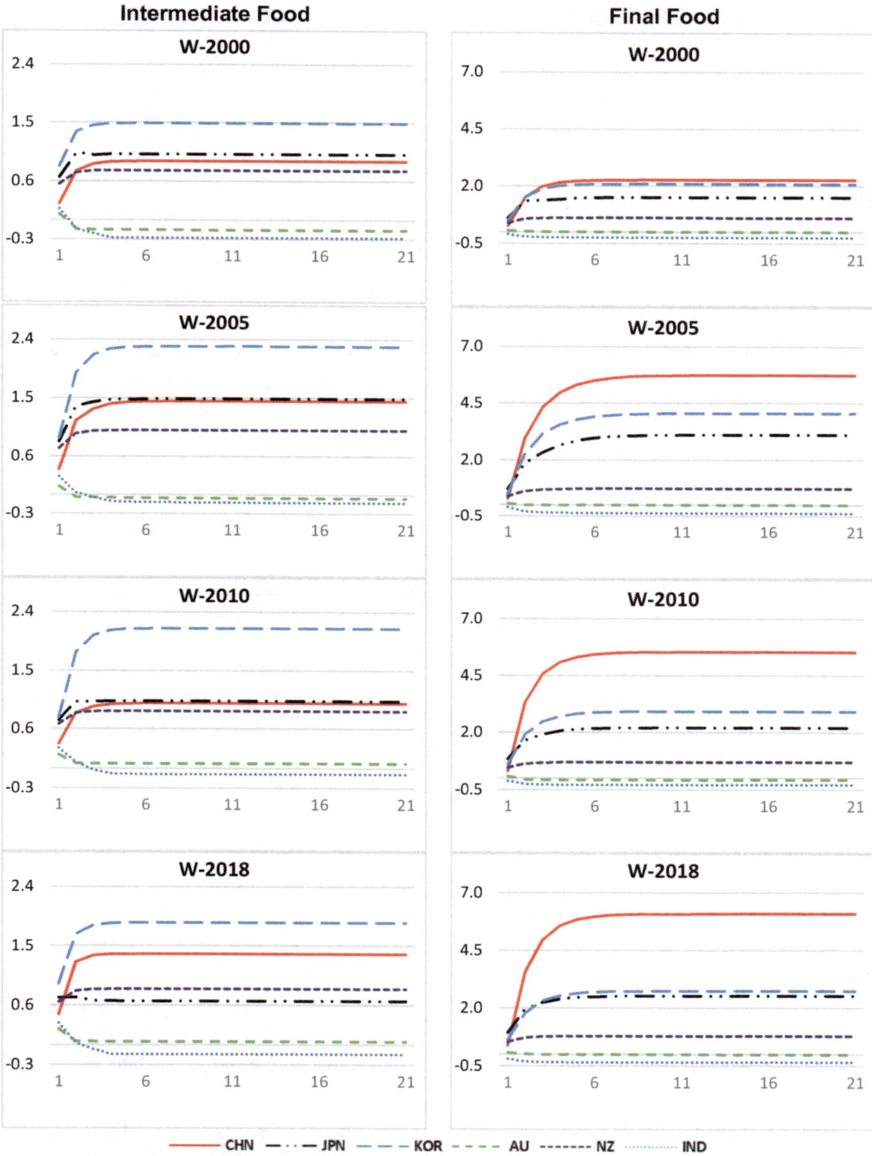

Fig. 4.9 Cumulative impulse responses of ASEAN6 to non-ASEAN RCEP, with different weights of intermediate food and final food. *Notes* The horizontal axis represents quarters, while the vertical axis shows the cumulative response to a one-unit output shock in the non-ASEAN RCEP members with different weights of intermediate food and final food respectively. See Table A.1 for country codes. *Source* Authors' own estimation

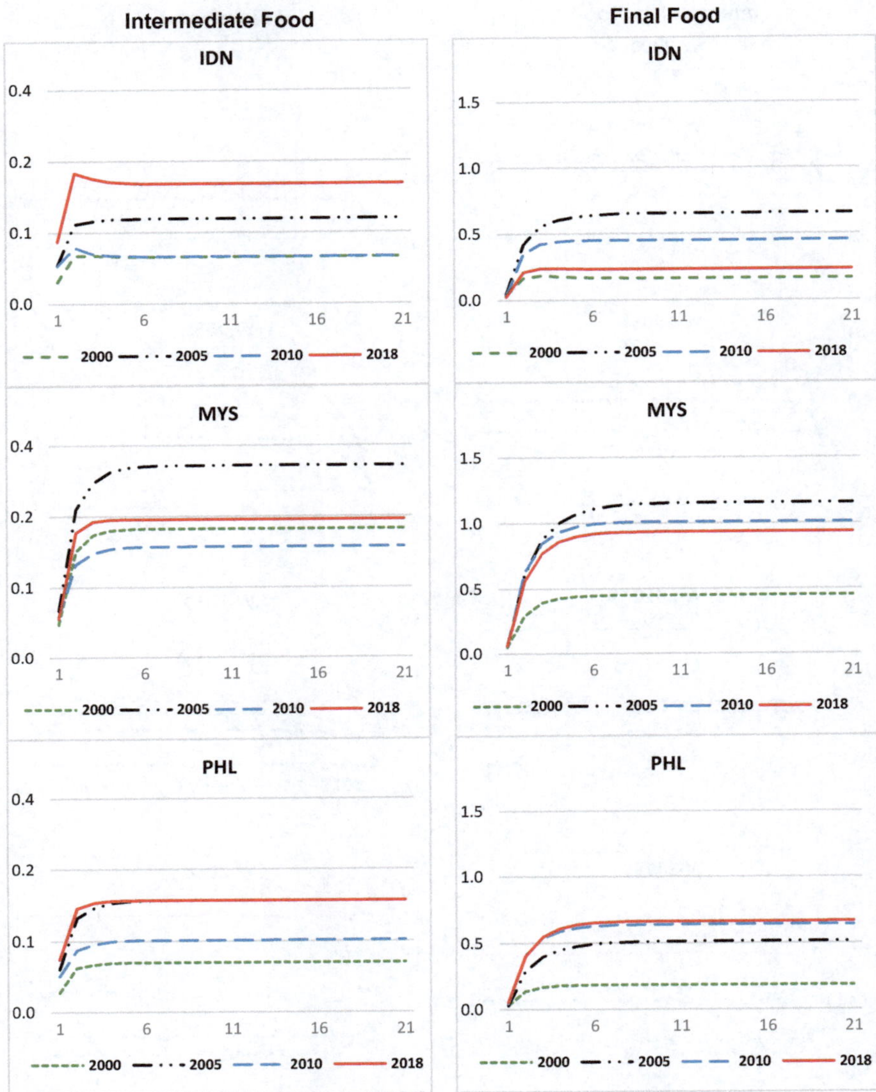

Fig. 4.10 Cumulative impulse responses of ASEAN6 to China, with different weights of intermediate food and final food. *Notes* The horizontal axis represents quarters, while the vertical axis shows the cumulative response to a one-unit output shock in China with different weights of intermediate food and final food respectively. See Table A.1 for country codes. *Source* Authors' own estimation

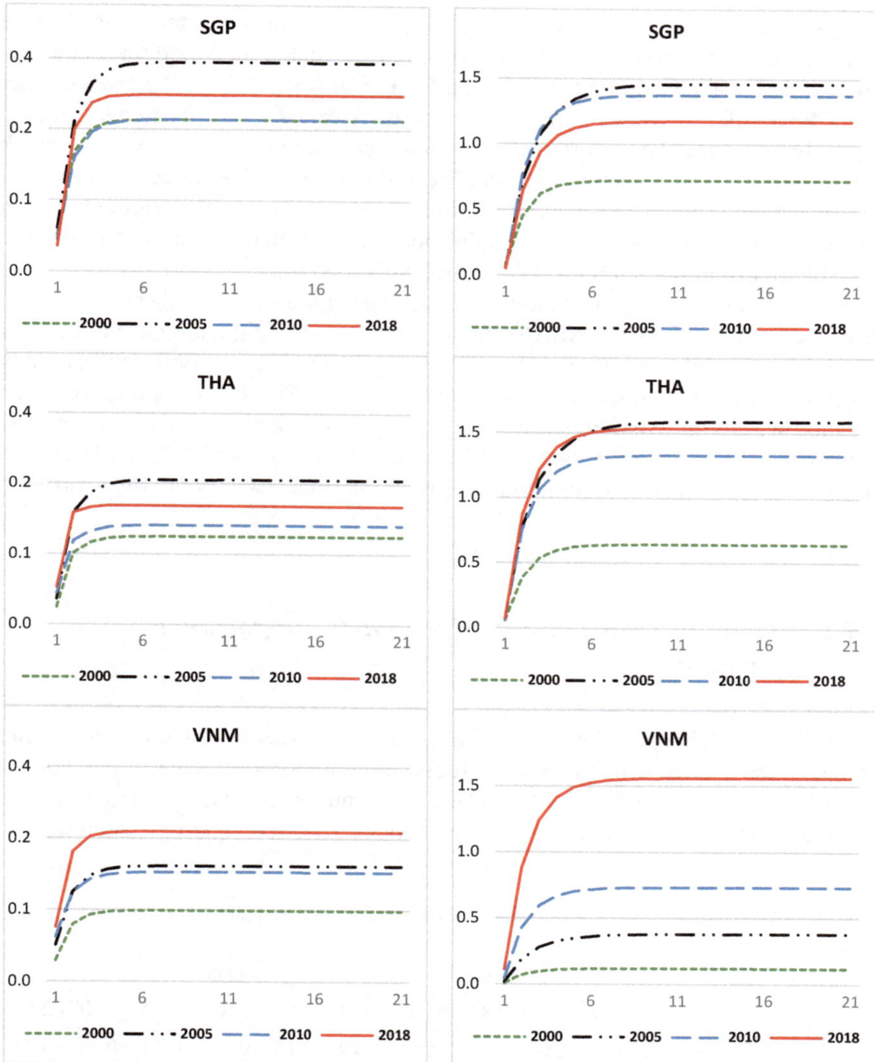

Fig. 4.10 (continued)

As for final food exports (right panel of Fig. 4.9), the responses of ASEAN6 to the externally generated one-unit shocks were larger than those for intermediate food. It also followed a slightly different response to shocks originating from the non-ASEAN RCEP countries. Here, an output shock from China relative to South Korea had a greater impact on ASEAN6, almost three times larger than if it is penetrating through the intermediate food channel. A significant jump in response of ASEAN6 to the Chinese shock was observed from 2005, compared to responses to shocks generated using 2000 weights. This highlights the rising importance of Chinese output shock transmissions to ASEAN6 economies via the final food trade channel. Though the bilateral export shares of final food from ASEAN6 to Japan were higher than China (refer to Fig. 4.6), the effects of a shock from China appeared larger than Japan, highlighting the importance of the indirect trade linkages that work through the third markets. In general, we also observed that the ASEAN6 economies were less sensitive to shocks in Australia and India, compared to shocks originating from the three East Asian economies. A notable observation is that New Zealand appeared to be the fourth important market for ASEAN6's food trade.

Since China is the key player in the ASEAN6 economies, we further explored the responses of the individual ASEAN6 economies to shocks originating from China for the four trade weights mentioned above. As shown in Figs. 4.10, a China output shock transmitted via the food trade link mattered more for ASEAN6 using the later trade weights. We interpret this evidence as suggesting that both direct and indirect effects contribute to the stronger impact of a China output shock on ASEAN countries, and the indirect channel of transmission is at least as important as the more obvious direct links.

4.5.2 *Dynamic Transmission Mechanism: Importance of China*

Tables 4.2 and 4.3 report the output multipliers for shocks from China, Japan, and Korea, as these three economies were found to be important growth drivers of the ASEAN6 for the last two decades. The output multipliers were estimated as the cumulative impulse responses to external shocks after four quarters, showing the

Table 4.2 Accumulated impact of growth drivers on ASEAN6, based on W-matrix of intermediate food

ASEAN6	CHN				JPN				KOR			
	2000	2005	2010	2018	2000	2005	2010	2018	2000	2005	2010	2018
IDN	0.08	0.14	0.08	0.21	0.09	0.22	0.19	0.15	0.21	0.35	0.34	0.37
MYS	0.22	0.32	0.18	0.23	0.24	0.34	0.19	0.08	0.35	0.54	0.45	0.29
PHL	0.08	0.18	0.12	0.19	0.04	0.08	0.04	0.03	0.12	0.22	0.29	0.27
SGP	0.25	0.34	0.25	0.30	0.30	0.38	0.27	0.15	0.38	0.54	0.44	0.28
THA	0.15	0.24	0.17	0.20	0.19	0.26	0.20	0.13	0.22	0.33	0.31	0.30
VNM	0.12	0.19	0.18	0.25	0.14	0.20	0.14	0.12	0.20	0.27	0.29	0.33
Average	**0.15**	**0.23**	**0.16**	**0.23**	**0.17**	**0.25**	**0.17**	**0.11**	**0.25**	**0.38**	**0.35**	**0.31**

Notes The rows indicate the responses of ASEAN6 to shocks that arise in the growth driver economies (China, Japan, and South Korea), as given in the columns. See Table A.1 for country codes

Source Authors' own estimation

Table 4.3 Accumulated impact of growth drivers on ASEAN6, based on W-matrix of final food

ASEAN6	CHN				JPN				KOR			
	2000	2005	2010	2018	2000	2005	2010	2018	2000	2005	2010	2018
IDN	0.17	0.60	0.44	0.23	−0.25	0.07	0.02	0.08	0.21	0.46	0.25	0.17
MYS	0.43	1.00	0.93	0.86	0.34	0.56	0.37	0.35	0.39	0.70	0.47	0.37
PHL	0.18	0.45	0.59	0.61	−0.01	0.16	0.19	0.20	0.16	0.31	0.33	0.28
SGP	0.68	1.25	1.25	1.06	0.62	0.74	0.53	0.47	0.64	0.88	0.61	0.46
THA	0.59	1.34	1.20	1.39	0.67	0.99	0.65	0.62	0.53	0.98	0.68	0.58
VNM	0.11	0.32	0.67	1.41	0.06	0.14	0.30	0.67	0.09	0.23	0.38	0.67
Average	**0.36**	**0.83**	**0.85**	**0.93**	**0.24**	**0.44**	**0.34**	**0.40**	**0.34**	**0.59**	**0.45**	**0.42**

Notes The rows indicate the responses of ASEAN6 to shocks that arise in the growth driver economies (China, Japan, and South Korea), as given in the columns. See Table A.1 for country codes
Source Authors' own estimation

accumulated impact of a one-unit expansion in the GDP of the driver economies on the output growth of the ASEAN6 economies transmitting through intermediate food and final food linkages. Both tables capture not only how a shock to the three growth driver economies directly affects the ASEAN6 economies, but also how the initial shock to one economy spreads through a chain of output effects in other countries. We found that the multiplier effects portrayed a different picture of the transmission of shocks than that provided by the bilateral trade flows between the 12 economies.

The four different year columns in Tables 4.2 and 4.3 take account of the different weights—2000, 2005, 2010 and 2018. The rows in those same tables show the impact on output growth of ASEAN6 economies, due to the shock originating in the growth driver economies indicated in the column. We analyze the responses of the ASEAN6 to two different trade channels, intermediate food, and final food, to capture the time varying effects of the extra-regional shocks.

From Table 4.2, we can clearly see that the propagation patterns by which the ASEAN6 economies responded to the growth drivers had changed over time. The big jump was observed using the 2005 trade weights, with South Korea recording the largest overall impact on the region. In 2005, the response of Malaysia and Singapore to output shocks from South Korea were 0.54 each. However, the responses of both countries fell to 0.28 and 0.29 respectively, when using the 2018 weights. The overall response of the ASEAN6 demonstrates that China is not the key player in intermediate food linkages.

The cumulative average impact of China's shock on ASEAN6 via the final food trade channel (as reported in Table 4.3) had increased to 0.93 from 0.36 (almost three times), confirming the importance of China as a major driver for ASEAN6's final food exports. Of this, Viet Nam, Thailand, and Singapore experienced the largest multiplier effects for 2018 trade weights, at 1.41, 1.39 and 1.06 respectively. The responses of those economies demonstrated that China is a key player in final food trade in the ASEAN region.

Tables 4.4 and 4.5 further report the normalized output multipliers, and they show the impact of a one percent positive output growth shock in an economy on the growth of its trading partner in the sample, for the given 2018 weights. It allows us to compare the significance of trading partners in the transmission of output shocks

Table 4.4 Normalized output-multipliers, based on 2018 W-matrix of intermediate food

	IDN	MYS	PHL	SGP	THA	VNM	CHN	JPN	KOR	AU	NZ	IND
IDN	1.00	0.28	−0.02	0.38	0.80	0.19	0.11	0.12	0.26	0.04	0.16	−0.38
MYS	0.28	1.00	0.01	0.31	0.36	0.17	0.13	0.06	0.20	0.00	0.15	−0.42
PHL	0.17	0.21	1.00	0.18	0.21	0.12	0.10	0.02	0.19	0.00	0.11	−0.09
SGP	0.24	0.30	−0.02	1.00	0.11	0.15	0.17	0.13	0.19	−0.01	0.10	−0.18
THA	0.27	0.20	−0.02	0.24	1.00	0.16	0.11	0.11	0.21	0.00	0.10	−0.15
VNM	0.19	0.24	0.00	0.25	0.21	1.00	0.14	0.10	0.23	0.02	0.10	−0.21
CHN	0.52	0.59	0.12	0.59	0.52	0.36	1.00	0.25	0.45	0.06	0.37	−0.27
JPN	0.35	0.40	0.10	0.53	0.42	0.31	0.26	1.00	0.60	0.02	0.17	−0.21
KOR	0.19	0.20	0.01	0.22	0.16	0.18	0.18	0.12	1.00	0.01	0.09	−0.17
AU	0.17	0.15	0.05	0.22	0.09	0.12	0.15	0.09	0.14	1.00	0.12	−0.04
NZ	0.08	0.08	0.01	0.04	0.02	0.05	0.18	0.03	0.06	0.04	1.00	−0.22
IND	0.43	0.43	0.02	0.26	0.42	0.19	0.11	0.07	0.19	0.02	0.11	1.00

Notes The columns indicate the responses of economies to a 1% positive output growth shock that originates in the given economies listed in the rows. See Table A.1 for country codes
Source Authors' own estimation

Table 4.5 Normalized output-multipliers, based on 2018 W-matrix of final food

	IDN	MYS	PHL	SGP	THA	VNM	CHN	JPN	KOR	AU	NZ	IND
IDN	1.00	0.15	−0.08	0.14	0.03	0.04	0.06	0.04	0.10	−0.02	0.06	−0.06
MYS	0.19	1.00	0.03	0.22	0.18	0.20	0.21	0.17	0.21	−0.02	0.11	−0.06
PHL	0.19	0.22	1.00	0.22	0.21	0.17	0.15	0.10	0.16	0.00	0.09	−0.04
SGP	0.24	0.47	0.05	1.00	0.21	0.27	0.26	0.23	0.26	0.01	0.12	−0.05
THA	0.22	0.35	0.07	0.24	1.00	0.32	0.35	0.30	0.33	0.01	0.12	−0.05
VNM	0.31	0.45	0.09	0.45	0.51	1.00	0.35	0.33	0.38	0.01	0.16	−0.12
CHN	0.57	0.78	0.32	0.64	1.05	0.83	1.00	0.68	0.81	0.08	0.56	−0.13
JPN	0.45	0.61	0.33	0.54	0.94	0.59	0.59	1.00	0.74	0.05	0.31	−0.10
KOR	0.19	0.27	0.16	0.21	0.32	0.28	0.29	0.30	1.00	0.02	0.14	−0.04
AU	0.16	0.29	0.06	0.31	0.26	0.20	0.21	0.19	0.21	1.00	0.24	−0.03
NZ	0.06	0.09	0.03	0.05	0.05	0.09	0.18	0.10	0.11	0.10	1.00	−0.01
IND	0.04	0.04	0.01	0.06	0.03	0.01	0.02	0.02	0.02	0.01	0.01	1.00

Notes The columns indicate the responses of economies to a 1% positive output growth shock that originates in the given economies listed in the rows. See Table A.1 for country codes
Source Authors' own estimation

between the 12 economies. The results illustrate the changing nature of international trade patterns across the two categories of trade exports—intermediate food and final food—and the significance of incorporating these changes while examining the global interdependencies.

The columns in Tables 4.4 and 4.5 indicate the responses of the economies to a one percent positive output growth shock that originates in the given economies listed in the rows. For instance, a one percent output shock from China triggered a 0.52% response in Thailand, while a one percent output shock from Thailand triggered only a 0.11% response in China. Across the ASEAN6, the impact of a one percent shock in China prompted responses only between 0.12% and 0.59%, with Malaysia and Singapore incurring the largest impact, while the Philippines, the lowest. Unlike final food (Table 4.5), India's output shock appeared to be transmitted via the intermediate food channel, triggering 0.43% responses each from Indonesia and Malaysia, and 0.42% from Thailand. In the case of intermediate food, the influence of the Chinese shock was also important for South Korea and New Zealand, with a response rate of 0.45% and 0.37% respectively. Overall, China's responses to shocks originating from ASEAN6, from both the intermediate food and final food channels, were less compared to its own influence on these economies.

China transmitted larger growth shocks via the final food channel (Table 4.5), where the average impact was higher compared to the impact coming through intermediate food trade channel. The impact of a one percent shock in China prompted responses between 0.32% and 1.05% across the ASEAN6. The second important growth driver in the region was Japan. Amongst the non-ASEAN RCEP economies, shocks from Japan and South Korea had the largest impact on China, 0.68%, and 0.81% respectively. In addition, there was also a strong interdependence between Japan and China, where China's response to South Korea was 0.59%. Zooming in on the intra-ASEAN6 relationships, we found Viet Nam had a larger influence on the ASEAN6 via the final food trade channel. Malaysia and Singapore experienced greater interdependence within the ASEAN6 region, while the Philippines remained less integrated in the region.

Tables 4.6 and 4.7 report the output growth co-movements within ASEAN6 and illustrates the effects of shocks penetrating through the food trade channels within the regional group. Overall, the effects on ASEAN6 from intra-regional output shocks appeared to be limited. However, greater cooperation and output growth co-movements were observed between Singapore with Indonesia, Malaysia, and Thailand. It showed that the multiplier effects of ASEAN6 (except Viet Nam) on the output growth of other ASEAN6 economies peaked in 2005, and thereafter the effects started to decline. A similar pattern was observed across the two categories of goods. However, if we compared the recent weights with 2000 weights, the intra-ASEAN6 growth interdependence had increased, reflecting their strengthened business cycle synchrony via the food trade channel.

Table 4.6 Intra-ASEAN6 output co-movements for intermediate food

ASEAN6	IDN				MYS				PHL			
	2000	2005	2010	2018	2000	2005	2010	2018	2000	2005	2010	2018
IDN	1.35	1.45	1.52	1.77	0.25	0.24	0.20	0.45	0.09	0.12	0.05	−0.02
MYS	0.43	0.55	0.55	0.50	1.89	1.72	1.57	1.61	0.13	0.25	0.09	0.01
PHL	0.08	0.14	0.18	0.29	0.18	0.18	0.19	0.34	0.93	0.96	0.94	0.91
SGP	0.40	0.44	0.40	0.42	0.88	0.59	0.43	0.48	0.11	0.15	0.05	−0.02
THA	0.15	0.23	0.30	0.47	0.31	0.33	0.24	0.32	0.02	0.06	0.04	−0.02
VNM	0.10	0.16	0.22	0.34	0.22	0.23	0.25	0.38	0.01	0.05	0.03	0.00
ASEAN6	SGP				THA				VNM			
	2000	2005	2010	2018	2000	2005	2010	2018	2000	2005	2010	2018
IDN	0.08	0.21	0.22	0.43	0.24	0.32	0.48	0.75	0.18	0.15	0.15	0.26
MYS	0.37	0.30	0.33	0.35	0.35	0.52	0.38	0.33	0.28	0.24	0.22	0.22
PHL	0.05	0.06	0.13	0.20	0.21	0.20	0.20	0.19	0.14	0.13	0.12	0.16
SGP	1.09	1.11	1.14	1.13	0.23	0.24	0.18	0.11	0.30	0.19	0.19	0.19
THA	0.04	0.07	0.12	0.28	0.92	0.94	0.94	0.93	0.16	0.15	0.15	0.21
VNM	0.02	0.07	0.12	0.28	0.09	0.18	0.20	0.19	1.24	1.25	1.26	1.32

Notes The rows indicate the responses of the individual ASEAN6 economies due to shocks in other members listed in the columns with the given W-matrices of intermediate goods. See Table A.1 for the country codes
Source Authors' own estimation

4.6 Conclusion

This chapter extends the analysis of Chap. 3 to take on a sectoral perspective in evaluating the transmission of output shocks of China on ASEAN6. It evaluates the role of bilateral food trade links *via* intermediate goods, and final goods in the international propagation of economic instabilities, using quarterly data on 12 economies (ASEAN6 and non-ASEAN RCEP) for the period 1995 to 2018. The same trade-linked VAR framework, detailed in Chap. 3, with time varying weights (2000, 2005, 2010 and 2018) are also applied for the empirical analyses in this chapter. The results were consistently reported for the propagation mechanism between economies through two types of cross-border channels—direct trade links and indirect third market links.

Some stylized facts are observed from the China–ASEAN engagement in food trade. The ASEAN region is not a major market for China's food trade. The nature of engagement between the two is mainly through final food or rather food for consumption, instead of intermediate food. ASEAN is however positioned in an increasingly problematic way within the regional food system despite being a net exporter of food to China. This comes from China's growing export food orientation and its shifts in food consumption patterns, followed by ASEAN's increasing food export dependency on China. Additionally, though China has a lower incidence of

Table 4.7 Intra-ASEAN6 output co-movements for final food

ASEAN6	IDN				MYS				PHL			
	2000	2005	2010	2018	2000	2005	2010	2018	2000	2005	2010	2018
IDN	1.44	1.51	1.41	1.37	0.31	0.47	0.32	0.22	0.05	0.08	0.02	−0.08
MYS	0.34	0.39	0.29	0.26	1.60	1.63	1.56	1.49	0.08	0.10	0.06	0.03
PHL	0.11	0.15	0.19	0.26	0.18	0.23	0.32	0.32	1.04	1.05	1.05	1.04
SGP	0.62	0.54	0.40	0.33	1.06	0.91	0.82	0.70	0.15	0.12	0.09	0.05
THA	0.36	0.38	0.31	0.29	0.44	0.56	0.54	0.52	0.12	0.15	0.11	0.08
VNM	0.06	0.11	0.23	0.42	0.09	0.13	0.36	0.66	0.01	0.02	0.04	0.09
ASEAN6	SGP				THA				VNM			
	2000	2005	2010	2018	2000	2005	2010	2018	2000	2005	2010	2018
IDN	0.10	0.27	0.17	0.16	0.10	0.15	0.10	0.04	0.11	0.11	0.08	0.07
MYS	0.16	0.27	0.28	0.25	0.28	0.28	0.20	0.21	0.14	0.17	0.21	0.34
PHL	0.07	0.11	0.19	0.25	0.10	0.14	0.21	0.25	0.08	0.13	0.26	0.29
SGP	1.08	1.11	1.13	1.14	0.47	0.31	0.25	0.24	0.26	0.18	0.27	0.46
THA	0.12	0.22	0.29	0.27	1.15	1.19	1.14	1.17	0.13	0.17	0.24	0.54
VNM	0.00	0.06	0.26	0.51	0.03	0.05	0.19	0.60	1.17	1.19	1.29	1.71

Notes The rows indicate the responses of the individual ASEAN6 economies due to shocks in other members listed in the columns with the given W-matrices of intermediate goods. See Table A.1 for the country codes
Source Authors' own estimation

NTMs in the food sector relative to ASEAN, the regulatory dissimilarity of China is considerably high when compared to the world average. This could impose significant trade costs for ASEAN and pose a barrier to China–ASEAN trade.

By focusing on the highly regulated food sector, the empirical analysis provides some intuition for understanding the possible interactions between trade policy and trade flows, though the former is not captured in the modelling exercise. The preliminary analysis of the trade links, traced through export shares between China and ASEAN, suggest a growing trade integration between China and ASEAN in both channels of food trade, intermediate food, and final food. Hence, the importance of food trade in the China–ASEAN engagement cannot be dismissed. The impulse response results suggest the importance of both the direct and indirect channels for the transmission of output shocks from China to ASEAN, and support the trade link analysis of a growing business synchrony between China and ASEAN in food trade in recent times. It also showcases the fact that China has a more influential impact on ASEAN's economic activity through the food trade channel than the other way around.

The empirical results based on the food sector in this chapter, interestingly, also provide some contradictory findings from that which was obtained in Chap. 3 for total merchandise goods. First, the South Korean (and not China) shock generated a larger impact on ASEAN through the intermediate food channel despite its lower trade intensities with ASEAN relative to China. The output multiplier effects further support the fact that China is not the key growth driver for ASEAN through the intermediate food trade linkages. Second, the final food (and not the intermediate food) is more important, and China propagated the largest impact on ASEAN through this channel. Here again, the output multiplier effects reinforce the role of China as the major growth driver for the propagation of output shocks through the final food trade channel.

References

Cadot, O., Asprilla, A., Gourdon, J., Knebel, C., & Peters, R. (2015). *Deep regional integration and non-tariff measures: A methodology for data analysis.* United Nations Conference on Trade and Development (UNCTAD): Geneva.

Cadot, O., & Ing, L. Y. (2015). Non-tariff measures and harmonization: Issues for the RCEP. ERIA Discussion Paper No. 2015-61. Economic Research Institute for ASEAN and East Asia (ERIA): Jakarta.

Chandra, A.C., & Lontoh, L.A. (2010). Regional food security and trade policy in Southeast Asia: The role of ASEAN. *Series on Trade and the Food Security – Policy Report 3,* International Institute for Sustainable Development (IISD): Manitoba.

Devadason, E. S., Chandran, V. G. R., & Kalirajan, K. (2018). Harmonization of food trade standards and regulations in ASEAN: The case of Malaysia's food imports. *Agricultural Economics, 49,* 97–109.

Dy, R. T. (2015). Japan–ASEAN agri-food trade: What is the score? Philippine Daily Inquirer, April, 27. Retrieved from https://business.inquirer.net/190885/japan-asean-agri-food-trade-what-is-the-score.

Distefano, T., Laio, F., Ridolfi, L., & Schiavo, S. (2018). Shock transmission in the international food trade network. *PLoS ONE, 13*(8), e0200639.

Farsund, A. A., Daugbjerg, C., & Langhelle, O. (2015). Food security and trade: Reconciling discourses in the food and agriculture organization and the world trade organization. *Food Security, 7,* 383–391.

Fold, N., Neilson, J., & Pritchard, B. (2011). Being sandwiched: The reshaping of ASEAN–China food trade. In D. S. L. Jarvis, & A. Welch (Eds.), *ASEAN industries and the challenge from China.* (pp.180–209). Palgrave MacMillan: United Kingdom.

Gale, F., & Huang, K. (2007). Demand for food quantity and quality in China. Economic Research Report Number 32, United States Department of Agriculture (USDA): Washington DC. Retrieved from: https://www.ers.usda.gov/webdocs/publications/45698/11803_err32fm_1_.pdf?v=3543.3.

Ing, L. Y., Peters, R., & Cadot, O. (2019). *Regional integration and non-tariff measures in ASEAN.* Economic Research Institute for ASEAN and East Asia (ERIA): Jakarta.

McKinsey Global Institute (2019). *China and the world: Inside the dynamics of a changing relationship.* McKinsey Global Institute: Brussels.

Nabeshima, K., & Obashi, A. (2019). Regulatory dissimilarity: A first look at the newly collected non-tariff measure database. ERIA Discussion Paper Series No. ERIA-DP-2018-12. Economic Research Institute for ASEAN and East Asia (ERIA): Jakarta.

Smith, V. H., & Glauber, J. W. (2019). Trade, policy and food security. *Agricultural Economics, 51*(1), 159–171.

Sun, L. (2019). Why China should open its market to more food imports. Sixth Tone, November 10. Retrieved from https://www.sixthtone.com/news/1004820/why-china-should-open-its-market-to-more-food-imports#.

Tobin, M., & Power, J. (2019). The spoils of trade war: Asia's winners and losers in US–China clash, South China Morning Post, 18 May. Retrieved from https://www.scmp.com/week-asia/geopolitics/article/3010733/spoils-trade-war-asias-winners-and-losers-us-china-clash.
UNCTAD. (2015). *International classification of non-tarff measures*. Geneva: United Nations Conference on Trade and Development (UNCTAD).
van Tongeren, F., & Huang, J. (Eds.). (2004). *China's food economy in the early 21st century*. Agricultural Economics Research Institute (LEI): The Hague.

Online Databases

CEIC Database. (2020). Retrieved from https://www.ceicdata.com/en.
IMF. (2020). Direction of trade statistics (DOTS). Retrieved from https://data.imf.org/?sk=9D6028D4-F14A-464C-A2F2-59B2CD424B85.
UN Comtrade. (2020). Retrieved from https://comtrade.un.org/data/.
UNCTAD-TRAINS Database. (2021). Retrieved from: https://trains.unctad.org/Default.aspx.
World Bank. (2020). World development indicators. Retrieved from https://databank.worldbank.org/source/world-development-indicators.

Chapter 5
Conclusion

5.1 China and ASEAN

Productions chains, represented by the surge of trade in intermediate and capital goods, reshaped regional trade, and changed the relationships within the AMS, and between the AMS and extra-regional partners. It is therefore well established that ASEAN's business cycles are synchronized through regional trade linkages. The rise of China as the world's manufacturing factory, however, added a twist to the regional production chain story as it accelerated the trade interdependence of the AMS with China, and also shifted the economic interdependence from one that is Japan-centered to China-centered, particularly in post 2005. China's interactions with the region intensified through trade in intermediate goods, displacing Japan's connection as a lead player with the region through the same trade flows. Though China remains a dominant player in the regional production chains, it is worth noting that the relationships between China and the AMS have also changed over time. China is also gaining ground as an exporter of consumption goods to ASEAN, and therefore the bilateral trade integration between China and ASEAN is no longer confined solely to the production chain story.

The issue of "interdependence", the degree to which economic conditions in China influences or harms the AMS, therefore becomes central to understanding the vulnerability of the latter. This volume investigates the observed transmission of economic fluctuations from China to the trade-linked ASEAN region. The trade channel is the focal point for understanding the propagation of economic output shocks in ASEAN as intraregional trade is the main factor pulling interdependence. To derive a better interpretation of the China-ASEAN transmission mechanisms, the trade channel accounts for the compositional effects, the origin of the shocks and time-varying effects. In focusing on the role of intermediate goods trade, this volume also adds to a recent literature, by quantifying the role of intermediate goods in the transmission of output shocks across borders.

M. Raghavan et al., *China and ASEAN: Pivoting Trade and Shock Transmission*,
https://doi.org/10.1007/978-981-16-1618-1_5

The findings of the study are discussed and interpreted in the next section by formalizing some intuitions about the way economic output of ASEAN and the individual AMS respond to demand changes in China vis-à-vis the other extra regional trading partners (the non-ASEAN RCEP members). The final section concludes with some new insights into the cross-border transmission patterns, and economic vulnerability and resilience of the AMS.

5.2 Interpretation of Findings

This section relates the empirical findings of Chaps. 3 and 4, namely the empirical analyses on trade links based on export shares, impulse responses, output multiplier effects, and output growth co-movements with the qualitative data analysis of Chap. 2, to draw meaningful interpretations and implications of the findings. Specifically, it provides answers to the questions raised in Chap. 1, reiterated here:

- How does ASEAN react to output shocks?
- What are the main trade channels behind the transmission of China's output shocks to ASEAN?
- How has China's growing engagement with ASEAN altered the transmission of output shocks to the region?
- How does China's role in the transmission of output shocks differ from shocks originating in other extra-regional trade partners of ASEAN?
- How does the trade channel further our understanding of what shapes the co-movement between China and the region, and China's influence as an exporter of shocks to the region?

Though the empirical analyses were confined to the ASEAN6, this sub-group is taken as representative of the entire ASEAN region given their importance in the regional production chain and their established trade linkages with China. Therefore, the following discussion and interpretation of the findings will make references to ASEAN, instead of the ASEAN6.

Overall, ASEAN displayed strong and rising output co-movements with the East Asian (China, Japan, and South Korea) trading partners, relative to Australia, New Zealand, and India. Within ASEAN, the macroeconomic interdependence with China, based on output co-movements, was higher with Malaysia, Singapore, Thailand, and Indonesia. The former three countries are not just active participants of GVCs and have established trade connections with China, they have also maintained trade surpluses in their favour in engagement with China. This generally supports the argument that greater trade integration stimulates the spillover of aggregate demand shocks, and thereby increasing output co-movement. In the case of Indonesia, which is less integrated in production chains, evidentially, the observed co-movement with China goes beyond economic activity to other factors of influence, such as liquidity conditions originating from the Chinese economy (Harahap et al. 2020). Hence, the trade channel, which is the focus of this volume, may not solely explain the cross-country linkages between China and Indonesia.

The intra-regional and inter-regional export shares suggest that, overall, the ASEAN6 is more integrated within the region and with the extra-regional (non-ASEAN RCEP) trade partners through intermediate goods relative to consumption goods. Having said that, the asymmetric interdependence between the AMS and China, reflected by the differences in the level of export integration, export commodity concentration, export market dependency, and export exposure (including the direct and indirect mechanisms; detailed below) account for the dissimilar impacts of China's output shocks on the region. Further, the close connectivity between some AMS in intermediate trade, such as Singapore and Malaysia with the other ASEAN trading partners, is also influential in explaining the indirect transmission of shocks to the regional members following from a direct shock from China to both the two key AMS.

For merchandise goods, four major results on the China-ASEAN connections follow from the analyses on impulse responses, and output multiplier effects. First, the intermediate goods trade channel mattered more for the transmission of output shocks from China to the region relative to the consumption goods trade channel. Second, the responses of ASEAN6 to output shocks from China were more pronounced than regional shocks, and shocks emanating from the other non-ASEAN RCEP countries. Third, the increasing cumulative impact of China's output shock on ASEAN6 was congruous to the growing trade links and trade intensities observed between ASEAN and China over the 1995 to 2018 period. Fourth, China was a dominant growth driver for ASEAN, post 2010, followed by South Korea and Japan. Taken together, the results suggest that Chinese output shocks are dominant, particularly through the intermediate goods trade channel, and the economic resilience of the region to the Chinese shocks depended on the indirect effects, apart from the direct trade links.

The main message is that China has gained an upper hand over Japan and South Korea in expanding its influence over ASEAN through trade in intermediate goods. This follows from the formulation of the modelling exercise, where the trade channel is distinguished between intermediate trade and consumption trade based on their respective export weights. Over-reliance on a single country like China for trade in intermediate goods (components) leaves the AMS vulnerable to output shocks that are transmitted through the trade channels. While positive shocks from China trigger stabilizing effects for ASEAN, especially with the tumultuous global trading environment, this only reflects half-a-story of the business cycle synchrony. That is, a slowdown in China's growth can be potentially destabilizing for the region. Understanding the extent of the damage to an adverse output shock from China, goes beyond examining the direct trade dependency of the AMS's on China. It includes the extent of trade exposure (detailed below) to China. Considering that China is also vulnerable to abrupt changes in the other regional economies (Japan and South Korea), and the international environment, renders instability for the region. The region has already experienced destabilizing effects from the triangular trade patterns between China, ASEAN and third markets from outside the wider region of Asia, starting from the AFC, GFC, the US-China trade war (Crowley 2019) and the ongoing global pandemic.[27] The production chain story is the main reason for explaining how these events have raised the stakes for trade and economic growth in Southeast Asia.

The empirical results from this volume also suggest the importance of not just China, but the trilateral group (China, Japan, and South Korea) in propagating output shocks to ASEAN. ASEAN is less sensitive to output shocks originating in Australia, New Zealand, and India. Interestingly, an output shock originating from South Korea had a larger impact on ASEAN relative to Japan, though the Japanese market is a relatively more important market for both intermediate exports and consumption exports from ASEAN. The results clearly put into perspective that it is not only the ASEAN economies with greater export links (or high trade dependency) with China that should be more susceptible to its shocks. Instead, the result suggests the interplay of indirect trade effects that buttress this mechanism for the transmission of output shocks originating outside the region on ASEAN, through both the intermediate goods and consumption goods trade channels.

The role of the indirect mechanism for predicting the ASEAN responses to output shocks from China, Japan, and South Korea, through the trade channel, was even more apparent when specific cross-country linkages were considered. That means that though some AMS may have low direct trade dependency with China, such as Indonesia, they may indeed have high export exposure to the latter if indirect linkages are included. This again suggests that the indirect transmission mechanism cannot be ignored when examining the exposure and resilience of ASEAN to output shocks. Direct links alone may fail to accurately capture the total trade exposure of the region, and their resilience to external shocks beyond the region (see also Raghavan and Devadason 2020).

In the case of the China-Vietnam trade relationship, Vietnam had been largely impacted by the output shocks from China with the 2018 trade weights relative to the earlier weights. The findings also showed that within ASEAN, Vietnam reported the largest cumulative response to an output shock in China through the intermediate goods trade channel. This result corroborates with Vietnam's recent rise and participation in the regional production chains. Vietnam's increase in trade intensity with China follows from its large imports of intermediate inputs from the latter (Nguyen 2020) and Vietnam has now emerged as the largest trade partner of China (see Table 2.2). Apart from its integration with China through production chain linkages, and other factors, such as the close geographical proximity to China, the relatively cheap labour, and FDI inflow to Vietnam (World Bank 2020), given its attractive position as the leading destination for companies pursuing the "China Plus One" strategy (strategy of spreading production between China and a Southeast Asian country; Shih 2020), has contributed to its rise in the region.

The propagation patterns by which the ASEAN6 economies responded to the growth drivers had also changed over time. The 'China factor' has evidentially demonstrated its dominance as a growth driver for ASEAN since 2010 via the intermediate goods and consumption goods trade channel. Its role as a growth driver surpassed that of the 'ASEAN factor' and that of the other remaining non-ASEAN RCEP members in influencing economic activity in the region. Second to China, is South Korea, a keen contender relative to Japan in the ASEAN trade connections.

Despite ASEAN's smaller export intensities to South Korea relative to Japan, the cumulative response of the former was larger for shocks originating from South Korea relative to Japan.

China's responses to shocks originating from ASEAN were much smaller compared to its own influence on these economies. That is, ASEAN had less of an influence on economic activity in China. This is not surprising given the sheer economic size of China relative to ASEAN. Beyond trade dependency, the findings from this study, especially on the trade exposure of ASEAN to shocks originating from China via the direct and indirect mechanisms of the trade channel, seem to provide additional support to the debate on the dominance of China in ASEAN, and the shifts in trade relationships between the two. That is, the latter argument on a unidirectional dependence of ASEAN on China, as alluded to in Chap. 2, seems to be rather convincing given the empirical findings of this study.

For food, similar results on the transmission of output shocks were obtained as that for merchandise goods. That are, the importance of the direct and indirect channels for the transmission of output shocks from China to ASEAN, the growing business synchrony between China and ASEAN through food trade, and the more influential impact of China on ASEAN's economic activity than the other way round. However, additional insights were derived from the analyses based on the food trade transmission channel, which diverged from the findings based on the merchandise trade channel. As noted above, the aggregate results for merchandise goods suggest that, for shock transmission through trade, the intermediate goods channel was more important than the consumption goods channel. This is not the case—at least in the context of intermediate food products. Final food or food for consumption was more important for the transmission of output shocks from China, and accordingly, China was the key growth driver for ASEAN through the final food trade channel, but not the intermediate food trade channel. The result supports the observed export flows, where consumption food dominated intermediate food in the export shares of China to ASEAN (see Fig. 4.2). The South Korean shock generated a larger impact on ASEAN through the intermediate food channel despite the lower food trade dependency of ASEAN on South Korea relative to China.

Finally, an important inference can be made (based on the aggregate export data for total merchandise goods and the data on food) from the results on the propagation of output shocks, from China, other AMS, and other non-ASEAN RCEP members, through the trade channel on ASEAN. The role of the intermediate goods trade channel in the propagation of output shocks to ASEAN is sector, and not source specific.

While emphasizing the role of demand changes through output shocks in transmitting disturbances to ASEAN through trade, we do not downplay the role of increased trade frictions in explaining economic growth through trade, especially for the highly regulated food sector. These frictions, in the form of tariffs, non-tariff barriers (NTBs) and NTMs, increase trade costs and may well be quite important in accounting for the declines in trade, for which the framework for this volume does not capture. Costly imported intermediates are a barrier for production chain integration.

Given the above findings, we can no longer take on the one-sided view of China as an 'insulator' for ASEAN to external shocks emanating from the global trading environment. ASEAN must therefore prepare to manage trade challenges from China, which are no longer limited to China's ongoing rebalancing policy (that is China's lower reliance on imported intermediate goods), as often projected in the contemporary debate of China's influence on the region. Importantly, China's role as an "exporter of shocks" to the region should be given due attention. Further trade challenges for ASEAN can also be envisaged, especially once the ongoing trilateral FTA is concluded between China, Japan, and South Korea. This is because the existing evidence indicated a strong interdependence of South Korea and Japan with China. The wider East Asia is also important for ASEAN as the production chains are more regional (see World Bank 2020). The trade volume between the three East Asian countries is already poised to increase considerably because of tariff concessions and trade facilitation (see Tan et al. 2020) from the recently signed RCEP. With new trade opportunities, come new risks from the trade linkages with those economies. An additional risk from the evidence of this volume is that Japan and South Korea are both affected directly by China and indirectly through China's output shock transmission on the AMS. This, in turn, can further result in a backlash for other AMS that have strong trade linkages with Japan and South Korea.

To conclude, China still dominates in triggering growth (and slowdown, if it is an adverse shock) in the region, and will continue to remain as an attractive place to anchor production chains. As such, the ASEAN6 economies need to devise policies regarding their overdependence on the external growth drivers, not just China but also South Korea and Japan, to minimize the adverse effects of economic instabilities. Building redundancy into supplier networks is one way to safeguard against output shocks that could be transmitted across borders. It is also a balancing act for ASEAN to enhance its leverage over China. Hence, adopting a "China plus" approach to merchandise goods might be the best option for many countries seeking to reduce risk exposure, and dilute the "China threat" for the region. It may be in the interest of ASEAN to reorient or diversify its supply chains, and for the food sector, the focus should be on diversifying its markets for final food products. Whilst designing policies to eliminate or minimize the effects of undesirable disturbances, identifying the origin of shocks, the mechanisms of the trade channels via which these shocks propagate, and the sectoral specificity of the trade shocks are seemingly important and need to be considered by the relevant stakeholders.

5.3 New Insights

What is clear from the contributions in this volume is that, there are certain hallmarks of the China-ASEAN regional trade interactions. The close trade linkages observed in the region accentuates several points about cross-border transmission patterns:

- First, the trade channel is important for output co-movement, and therefore, the transmission patterns cannot merely be explained with the standard openness measures, such as export or trade shares. ***Intermediate goods linkages***, more specifically, which strengthen the synchronization of output fluctuations, were found to be more relevant for explaining the cross-border transmissions of output shocks from China to the highly connected ASEAN region. Hence, further distinguishing the trade channel into intermediate goods and consumption goods through the trade weights is highly relevant for examining the transmission of output shocks to ASEAN.
- Second, the intra-ASEAN trade interactions, and between ASEAN and the non-ASEAN RCEP (namely Japan and South Korea), provided additional influences when examining cumulative responses of ASEAN from an output shock in China. The cumulative impact of China's shock on some countries was not congruous to the observed (direct) trade dependency based on the trade links and trade intensities between them. Hence, the economic resilience of ASEAN to shocks originating in China depends on their total trade exposure to the latter, coming from the ***indirect effects***, apart from the direct trade links. The indirect mechanism must therefore be considered at least as important as the more obvious direct links.
- Third, the inclusion of ***time-varying weights*** indicated a strengthened business cycle synchrony between China and ASEAN over time, and more importantly with Viet Nam in recent times. The time dimension is important for understanding the changing influence of China on the region, and the corresponding responses of the AMS, especially through the trade in intermediate goods channel. This is relevant as China and some other AMS are already beginning to reassess their production chains, starting from the US-China trade war.
- Fourth, production chains better explain the heterogeneity observed on a country level, and not ***sectoral level***, indicating that other contributive factors may also have been at work to explain the diversity of the observed results in the food sector.

So, what might be the answer to the issue posed in this volume—whether China's trade engagement with ASEAN constitutes a changing order with possible risks. This volume forwards that there are certainly risks attached to the trade interdependence between China and ASEAN. Unique issues to the China-ASEAN relationship need to be accounted for. First, the intermediate trade channel for propagating output shocks from China to ASEAN; Second, the indirect effects for predicting responses of ASEAN to output shocks originating in China; Third, the time-varying effects for informing on the increasing dominance of China in ASEAN; and Fourth, the diversity of responses at the country-level and sectoral level to output shocks originating from China.

References

Crowley, M. A. (Ed.). (2019). *Trade war: The clash of economic systems endangering global prosperity*. London: Center for Economic Policy Research (CEPR) Press.

Harahap, B. A., Barry, P., & Kusuma, A. C. M. (2020). *Journal of Central Banking Theory and Practice*. https://doi.org/10.2478/jcbtp-2020-0029.

Nguyen, T. (2020). Is Vietnam eating into China's share of manufacturing? Retrieved June 18, from https://carnegieendowment.org/2020/06/18/is-vietnam-eating-into-china-s-share-of-manufacturing-pub-82094.

Raghavan, M., & Devadason, E. S. (2020). How resilient Is ASEAN-5 to trade shocks? A comparison of regional and global shocks. *Global Journal of Emerging Market Economies, 12*(1), 93–115.

Shih, W. C. (2020). Global supply chains in a post-pandemic world. *Harvard Business Review*. Retrieved September–October 2020, from https://hbr.org/2020/09/global-supply-chains-in-a-post-pandemic-world

Tan, I., Wu, D., Pan, J., & Weng, K. K. (2020). Understanding the regional comprehensive economic partnership agreement (RCEP)—What does the RCEP mean to businesses? Retrieved from https://www.bakermckenzie.com/-/media/files/insight/publications/2020/12/bakermckenzie_understandingrcep_dec2020.pdf?la=en

World Bank. (2020). *Trading for development in the age of global value chains*. Washington DC: World Bank.

Appendix

Tables A.1, A.2, A.3, A.4, A.5, A.6, A.7 and A.8.

Table A.1 Sample of countries

Country	Code
ASEAN6	
Indonesia	IDN
Malaysia	MYS
Philippines	PHL
Singapore	SGP
Thailand	THA
Viet Nam	VNM
Remaining AMS	
Brunei	BRN
Cambodia	KHM
Lao PDR	LAO
Myanmar	MMR
Non-ASEAN RCEP	
China	CHN
Japan	JPN
South Korea	KOR
Australia	AU
New Zealand	NZ
India	IND

M. Raghavan et al., *China and ASEAN: Pivoting Trade and Shock Transmission*, https://doi.org/10.1007/978-981-16-1618-1

Table A.2 Classification of capital, intermediate and consumption goods

BEC code	Description
Capital goods	
41	Capital goods (except transport equipment)
521	Transport equipment, industrial
Intermediate goods	
111	Food and beverages, primary, mainly for industry
121	Food and beverages, processed, mainly for industry
21	Industrial supplies not elsewhere specified, primary
22	Industrial supplies not elsewhere specified, processed
31	Fuels and lubricants, primary
321	Fuels and lubricants, processed (motor spirit)
322	Fuels and lubricants, processed (other than motor spirit)
42	Parts and accessories of capital goods (except transport equipment)
53	Parts and accessories of transport equipment
Consumption goods	
112	Food and beverages, primary, mainly for household consumption
122	Food and beverages, processed, mainly for household consumption
522	Transport equipment, non-industrial
51	Passenger motor cars
61	Consumer goods not elsewhere specified, durable
62	Consumer goods not elsewhere specified, semi durable
63	Consumer goods not elsewhere specified, non-durable

Note BEC—Broad Economic Categories is a reclassification of traded goods according to their main end use
Source UN Comtrade (2020)

Table A.3 AMS—Participation in global value chains, by FVA and DVX (%)

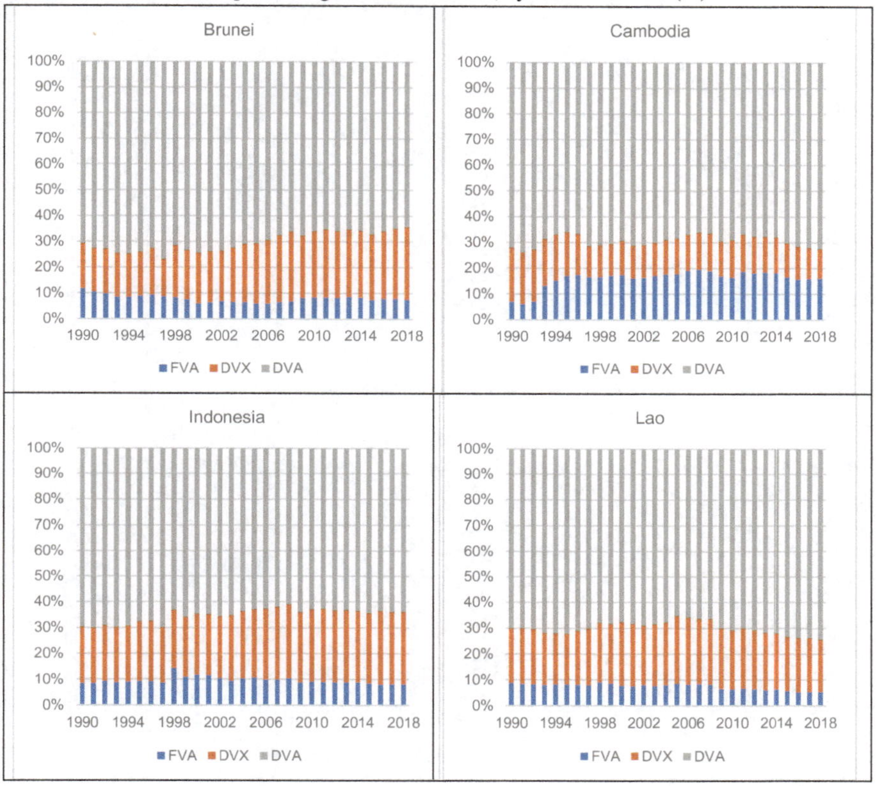

(continued)

Table A.3 (continued)

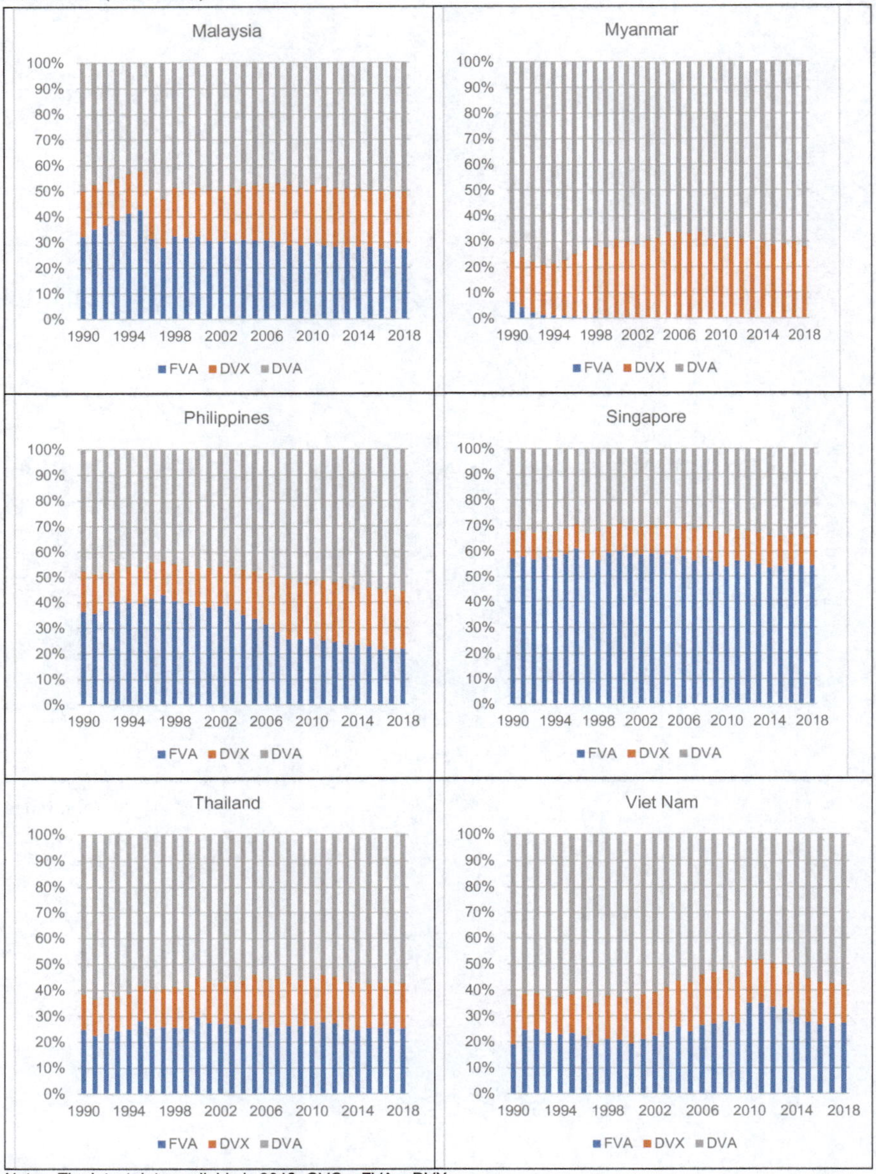

Notes: The latest data available is 2018. GVC = FVA + DVX.
Source: Calculated from UNCTAD-Eora GVC database (2020).

Table A.4 China and ASEAN—RCA indices for machinery and transport, 1995 and 2019

SITC Product	CHN		BRN		IDN		KHM		LAO		MMR		MYS		SGP		THA		PHL		VNM	
	1995	2019	1995	2019	1995	2019	1995	2019	1995	2019	1995	2019	1995	2019	1995	2019	1995	2019	1995	2019	1995	2019
[711] Vapour generating boilers, auxiliary plant; parts	0.45	2.38	0.02	0.20	0.10	0.35	..	0.03	..	0.02	..	0.02	0.24	0.83	0.28	0.21	0.01	0.61	0.03	0.59	0.00	1.14
[712] Steam turbines & other vapour turbin., parts, n.e.s.	0.07	1.29	0.74	0.07	0.05	0.39	..	..	..	0.00	..	0.09	0.11	0.15	0.66	0.23	0.03	0.30	..	0.60	..	0.01
[713] Internal combustion piston engines, parts, n.e.s.	0.16	0.49	0.07	0.18	0.03	0.58	0.01	0.00	0.00	0.01	0.01	0.09	0.17	0.07	0.25	0.82	0.16	2.14	0.01	0.05	0.02	0.08
[714] Engines & motors, non-electric; parts, n.e.s.	0.03	0.22	0.03	0.10	0.01	0.04	..	0.00	0.11	0.03	0.31	0.04	0.03	0.13	0.29	4.10	0.04	0.24	..	0.01	..	0.01
[716] Rotating electric plant & parts thereof, n.e.s.	1.45	1.57	0.08	0.05	0.30	0.29	..	0.83	..	0.03	0.03	0.08	1.32	0.21	1.68	0.66	1.51	0.93	0.02	0.82	0.19	0.99
[718] Other power generating machinery & parts, n.e.s.	0.22	0.80	0.02	0.05	0.00	0.07	0.02	0.07	..	0.00	0.07	0.27	0.05	0.19	0.22	0.54	0.02	0.40	0.00	0.23	0.10	0.03
[721] Agricultural machinery (excluding tractors) & parts	0.10	0.75	0.01	0.00	0.02	0.02	..	0.04	..	0.00	..	0.11	0.04	0.49	0.07	0.13	0.03	0.76	0.01	0.06	0.03	0.10
[722] Tractors (excluding those of 71414 & 74415)	0.28	0.22	..	0.00	0.00	0.37	0.04	0.03	0.13	0.01	..	0.04	0.01	0.03	0.03	0.03	0.04	1.15	0.00	0.00	0.06	0.06
[723] Civil engineering & contractors' plant & equipment	0.18	0.94	0.12	0.20	0.12	0.81	0.01	0.02	0.06	0.06	0.03	0.56	0.29	0.65	1.18	1.29	0.09	0.65	0.02	0.08	0.43	0.06
[724] Textile & leather machinery, & parts thereof, n.e.s.	0.55	1.89	0.01	0.00	0.03	0.11	0.02	0.14	0.40	0.01	0.01	0.07	0.09	0.63	0.32	1.04	0.15	1.67	0.03	0.05	0.63	3.06
[725] Paper mill, pulp mill machinery; paper articles man.	0.10	1.10	0.00	0.05	0.07	0.06	0.00	0.01	..	0.00	..	0.01	0.06	0.14	0.13	0.34	0.08	0.14	0.13	0.11	0.00	0.15
[726] Printing & bookbinding machinery, & parts thereof	0.07	0.46	0.00	0.05	0.05	1.41	..	0.05	0.03	0.00	..	0.00	0.07	0.87	0.23	0.96	0.05	0.23	0.03	1.93	0.00	0.20
[727] Food-processing machines (excluding domestic)	0.24	0.67	..	0.00	0.09	0.10	0.01	0.05	0.00	0.06	0.00	0.00	0.36	0.92	0.33	0.18	0.19	0.34	0.14	0.26	0.15	0.22
[728] Other machinery for particular industries, n.e.s.	0.23	0.65	0.02	0.05	0.20	0.09	0.04	0.01	0.00	0.04	0.04	0.05	0.24	0.99	0.60	2.43	0.11	0.17	0.03	0.24	0.07	0.12
[731] Machine-tools working by removing material	0.46	0.55	0.05	0.03	0.00	0.06	..	0.01	..	0.02	0.00	0.03	0.11	0.14	0.47	0.56	0.43	1.05	0.01	0.20	0.01	0.03
[733] Mach.-tools for working metal, excluding removing mate.	0.28	0.87	0.12	0.04	0.01	0.07	..	0.05	..	0.03	0.01	0.13	0.19	0.86	0.57	0.32	0.07	0.31	0.05	0.06	0.03	0.22
[735] Parts, n.e.s., & accessories for machines of 731, 733	0.32	0.43	0.00	0.02	0.00	0.13	..	0.02	..	0.02	0.03	0.01	0.13	1.47	0.40	0.72	0.18	0.56	0.35	1.05	0.00	0.22
[737] Metalworking machinery (excludingmachine-tools) & parts	0.30	1.30	0.07	0.23	0.05	0.07	..	0.06	..	0.12	0.00	0.09	0.22	0.20	0.41	0.28	0.20	0.52	0.03	0.19	0.01	0.06
[741] Heating & cooling equipment & parts thereof, n.e.s.	0.21	1.66	0.04	0.05	0.10	0.15	0.02	0.03	0.04	0.02	0.00	0.07	1.92	1.21	0.75	0.52	2.10	3.46	0.07	0.86	0.01	0.14
[742] Pumps for liquids	0.21	0.93	0.07	0.22	0.02	0.15	0.01	0.01	..	0.03	0.09	0.13	0.06	0.12	0.38	0.59	0.14	0.88	0.03	0.09	0.02	0.12
[743] Pumps (excluding liquid), gas compressors & fans; centrifugal	0.88	1.17	0.03	0.06	0.18	0.32	0.10	0.06	0.00	0.02	0.03	0.58	0.49	0.61	0.88	0.51	0.76	1.57	0.08	0.29	0.06	0.18
[744] Mechanical handling equipment, & parts, n.e.s.	0.41	1.36	0.13	0.25	0.06	0.06	0.01	0.02	0.12	0.01	0.03	0.25	0.22	0.32	0.51	0.32	0.31	0.53	0.01	0.07	0.01	0.12
[745] Other non-electrical machinery, tools & mechanical apparatus	0.14	1.21	0.05	0.03	0.09	0.14	0.00	0.05	0.00	0.05	0.01	0.01	0.16	0.27	0.33	0.34	0.07	0.30	0.05	0.15	0.04	0.10
[746] Ball or roller bearings	0.94	1.30	0.00	0.01	0.03	0.60	0.00	0.40	0.00	0.00	0.01	0.00	0.35	0.43	1.99	1.39	1.97	1.30	0.00	0.43	0.07	0.32
[747] Appliances for pipes, boiler shells, tanks, vats, etc.	0.37	1.35	0.09	0.07	0.11	0.11	0.00	0.00	0.01	0.01	0.03	0.01	0.07	0.33	0.35	0.67	0.24	0.62	0.04	0.49	0.00	0.62
[748] Transmis. shafts	0.50	1.04	0.01	0.02	0.05	0.29	0.00	0.01	0.01	0.01	0.07	0.00	0.06	0.18	0.48	0.38	0.15	0.57	0.04	0.64	0.01	0.24
[749] Non-electric parts & accessories of machinery, n.e.s.	0.22	1.53	0.82	0.01	0.08	0.27	0.04	0.02	..	0.00	0.00	0.03	0.53	0.75	0.91	0.70	0.74	0.74	0.10	0.21	0.15	0.28
[751] Office machines	1.81	1.94	0.03	0.02	0.55	0.15	0.00	0.01	0.01	0.01	0.00	0.01	0.98	1.23	1.30	0.58	2.69	3.62	0.03	11.80	0.01	5.66
[752] Automatic data processing machines, n.e.s.	0.59	2.90	0.03	0.01	0.14	0.46	0.06	0.04	..	0.09	0.00	0.01	1.13	1.80	6.89	1.12	1.93	2.62	0.59	3.51	0.01	1.05
[759] Parts, accessories for machines of groups 751, 752	0.57	2.04	0.01	0.02	0.29	0.23	0.00	0.18	0.00	1.08	0.00	0.05	3.33	1.52	3.90	1.69	2.14	1.05	0.51	1.39	0.00	1.94
[761] Television receivers, whether or not combined	1.18	2.57	0.01	0.03	0.16	1.13	0.25	0.08	0.00	0.00	0.01	0.00	6.57	1.72	2.84	0.33	3.66	1.23	0.88	0.29	0.68	1.95
[762] Radio-broadcast receivers, whether or not combined	3.96	2.36	0.02	0.01	2.64	1.26	0.01	0.00	0.00	0.01	0.03	0.00	10.89	3.63	3.90	0.14	0.07	4.70	1.58	0.80	0.06	0.48
[763] Sound recorders or reproducers	1.62	2.71	0.05	0.06	3.67	0.90	0.05	0.07	0.00	8.45	0.00	0.33	9.11	0.79	4.14	0.85	2.22	2.80	0.26	0.58	0.10	3.14
[764] Telecommunication equipment, n.e.s.; & parts, n.e.s.	1.15	2.86	0.08	0.02	0.36	0.17	0.03	0.08	0.03	1.96	0.08	0.08	2.17	0.82	2.29	0.85	1.15	0.54	1.44	0.66	0.34	6.76
[771] Electric power machinery, and parts thereof	2.25	1.99	0.07	0.01	0.33	0.49	0.00	0.82	0.19	0.32	0.07	0.17	1.58	0.60	1.67	0.67	2.17	1.24	0.40	4.80	0.42	1.10
[772] Apparatus for electrical circuits; board, panels	0.84	1.27	0.02	0.15	0.18	0.37	0.01	0.10	0.00	0.09	0.07	0.04	1.25	1.35	1.65	1.07	1.32	1.42	0.52	1.43	2.33	0.76
[773] Equipment for distributing electricity, n.e.s.	0.63	1.36	0.01	0.01	0.28	1.05	0.00	2.06	0.00	0.95	0.18	0.01	0.82	0.49	0.70	0.37	1.58	0.72	4.70	4.25	0.37	2.35
[774] Electro-diagnostic appliances for medical sciences, etc.	0.11	0.56	0.02	0.02	0.00	0.12	0.01	0.01	..	0.00	..	0.06	0.03	0.70	0.17	1.04	0.02	0.08	..	0.22	0.00	0.25
[775] Household type equipment, electrical or not, n.e.s.	1.52	2.77	0.02	0.02	0.05	0.72	0.01	0.07	0.03	0.07	0.00	0.21	0.51	1.11	0.72	0.16	1.63	2.51	0.30	0.15	0.10	0.50
[776] Cathode valves & tubes	0.24	1.19	0.01	0.02	0.09	0.09	0.01	0.02	..	0.03	0.00	0.01	4.93	5.43	3.98	4.72	1.43	1.20	2.50	6.25	0.21	1.06
[778] Electrical machinery & apparatus, n.e.s.	1.03	1.87	0.02	0.03	0.55	0.78	0.00	0.09	0.02	0.12	0.02	0.01	0.62	1.47	1.30	0.80	0.85	1.07	0.24	6.54	0.17	0.63
[781] Motor vehicles for the transport of persons	0.00	0.07	0.00	0.01	0.01	0.45	0.01	0.00	0.01	0.01	0.00	0.00	0.05	0.03	0.04	0.02	0.01	1.10	0.00	0.01	0.00	0.00
[782] Motor vehicles for transport of goods, special purpose	0.09	0.26	0.13	0.01	0.01	0.07	0.05	0.00	0.01	0.07	0.00	0.05	0.01	0.01	0.09	0.03	0.17	3.59	0.00	0.02	0.01	0.01
[783] Road motor vehicles, n.e.s.	0.02	0.48	0.01	0.01	0.01	0.15	0.01	0.00	..	0.00	0.00	0.12	0.01	0.24	0.05	0.05	0.00	0.09	0.04	0.00	..	0.01
[784] Parts & accessories of vehicles of 722, 781, 782, 783	0.12	0.64	0.01	0.00	0.05	0.57	0.00	0.04	0.00	0.00	0.00	0.02	0.05	0.18	0.12	0.23	0.11	1.51	0.54	0.79	0.00	0.24
[785] Motorcycles & cycles	1.64	2.26	0.01	0.00	1.51	2.93	0.47	5.78	41.08	0.02	0.00	0.01	0.49	0.60	0.95	0.65	1.94	2.67	0.39	0.34	0.36	1.75
[786] Trailers & semi-trailers	4.57	2.26	0.23	0.09	0.60	0.04	0.02	0.00	0.01	0.00	0.04	0.02	0.57	0.16	0.16	0.14	0.85	0.77	0.01	0.31	0.05	0.12
[791] Railway vehicles & associated equipment	0.31	0.78	0.00	0.00	0.00	0.05	0.00	0.00	..	0.01	..	0.02	0.01	0.04	0.03	0.04	0.01	0.01	0.01	0.01	0.04	0.01
[792] Aircraft & associated equipment; spacecraft, etc.	0.07	0.17	0.96	0.55	0.03	0.06	0.01	0.01	0.00	0.30	0.04	1.19	1.31	0.70	0.25	1.44	0.74	0.44	0.01	1.09	0.02	0.17
[793] Ships, boats & floating structures	0.81	1.40	2.50	0.06	0.27	0.18	..	0.01	0.00	0.00	0.04	0.74	0.63	0.19	1.07	0.59	0.18	0.78	0.00	1.65	0.15	0.46

Notes: CHN —China; BRN —Brunei; KHM —Cambodia; IDN —Indonesia; LAO —Lao, PDR; MMR —Myanmar; MYS —Malaysia; SGP —Singapore; THA —Thailand; PHL - Philippines; VNM —Viet Nam. The country has a comparative advantage in a product if its RCA > 1.
Source: Compiled from UNCTADstat (2020).

Table A.5 Descriptive statistics of GDP growth rate series (1995Q1 to 2018Q4)

	Mean	Median	Max	Min	Std. Dev	Observations
ASEAN6						
IDN	0.011	0.013	0.041	-0.108	0.017	95
MYS	0.012	0.014	0.039	-0.067	0.015	95
PHL	0.012	0.013	0.029	-0.030	0.009	95
SGP	0.013	0.012	0.060	-0.029	0.018	95
THA	0.008	0.009	0.085	-0.065	0.019	95
VNM	0.009	0.011	0.084	-0.038	0.022	95
Non-ASEAN RCEP						
CHN	0.021	0.020	0.044	0.001	0.007	95
JPN	0.002	0.003	0.025	-0.049	0.010	95
KOR	0.012	0.010	0.121	-0.060	0.017	95
AU	0.008	0.007	0.029	-0.005	0.005	95
NZ	0.006	0.007	0.025	-0.017	0.007	95
IND	0.016	0.016	0.067	-0.023	0.012	95

Note Refer to Table A.1 for country codes

Table A.6 Unit root tests of GDP growth rate series (1995Q1 to 2018Q4)

	KPSS			Phillips-Perron		
	h	*p*-value	t-stat	h	*p*-value	t-stat
ASEAN6						
IDN	0	0.100	0.069	1	0.001	−6.6108
MYS	0	0.100	0.029	1	0.001	−6.3574
PHL	0	0.100	0.036	1	0.001	−8.8735
SGP	0	0.100	0.061	1	0.001	−7.7009
THA	0	0.100	0.081	1	0.001	−9.5059
VNM	0	0.100	0.081	1	0.001	−7.8519
Non-ASEAN RCEP						
CHN	0	0.100	0.031	1	0.001	−7.5841
JPN	0	0.100	0.046	1	0.001	−8.3336
KOR	0	0.100	0.035	1	0.001	−7.2758
AU	0	0.100	0.043	1	0.001	−11.787
NZ	0	0.100	0.116	1	0.001	−8.1291
IND	0	0.100	0.066	1	0.001	−10.637

Note The null hypothesis of KPSS-test assumes that the variable is stationary and vice versa in Phillips–Perron. For KPSS, $h = 1$ represents rejection of H_0 (trend stationary) in favour of H_1 (unit root), whereas for PP-test, $h = 0$ shows failure to reject H_0. The C-values for KPSS and Phillips-Perron at the 5% level of significance are 0.146 and −3.459 respectively

Table A.7 Description of food and agriculture products, by HS codes

No.	Product description (HS 2-digit)
Food (Including beverages)	
1	02—Meat and edible meat offal
2	03—Fish and crustaceans, molluscs and other aquatic invertebrates
3	04—Dairy produce; bird's eggs; natural honey; edible products of animal origin, not elsewhere specific or included
4	07—Vegetables and certain roots and tubers; edible
5	08—Fruit and nuts, edible; peel of citrus fruits and melons
6	09—Coffee, tea, mate and spices
7	10—Cereals
8	11—Products of the milling industry; malt, starches, inulin, wheat gluten
9	12—Oil seeds and oleaginous fruits; miscellaneous grains, seeds and fruits, industrial or medicinal plants; straw and fodder
10	13—Lac; gums, resins and other vegetable saps and extracts
11	15—Animal or vegetable fats and oils and their cleavage products; prepared animal fats; animal or vegetable waxes
12	16—Meat, fish or crustaceans, molluscs or other invertebrates; preparations thereof
13	17—Sugars and sugar confectionery
14	18—Cocoa and cocoa preparations
15	19—Preparations of cereal, flour, starch or milk; pastry cooks' products
16	20—Preparations of vegetables, fruits, nuts or other parts of plants
17	21—Miscellaneous edible preparations
18	22—Beverages, spirits and vinegar
Agriculture (includes food and beverages)	
19	01—Animals, live
20	05—Animal originated products, not elsewhere specified or included
21	06—Trees and other plants, live; bulbs, roots and the like; cut flowers and ornamental foliage
22	14—Vegetable plaiting materials; vegetable products not elsewhere specified or included
23	23—Food industries, residues and wastes thereof; prepared animal fodder
24	24—Tobacco and manufactured tobacco substitutes

Table A.8
Intra-ASEAN—Regulatory distance of technical measures in agriculture

Country-Pair	SPS	TBT	INSP
BRN-IDN	0.2281	0.1190	0.2977
BRN-KHM	0.2175	0.2035	0.0554
BRN-LAO	0.2165	0.0695	0.3043
BRN-MMR	0.1931	0.0723	0.2688
BRN-MYS	0.1795	0.1096	0.0923
BRN-PHL	0.3364	0.1214	0.4035
BRN-SGP	0.1182	0.0744	0.0554
BRN-THA	0.2087	0.1376	0.0554
BRN-VNM	0.3004	0.0563	0.0674
IDN-KHM	0.1748	0.1950	0.3096
IDN-LAO	0.2394	0.0887	0.2899
IDN-MMR	0.2427	0.1292	0.5230
IDN-MYS	0.2434	0.1607	0.3354
IDN-PHL	0.3384	0.1348	0.5478
IDN-SGP	0.1858	0.1014	0.3096
IDN-THA	0.2732	0.1651	0.3096
IDN-VNM	0.2754	0.1060	0.3140
KHM-LAO	0.1928	0.1541	0.3300
KHM-MMR	0.2252	0.2200	0.2134
KHM-MYS	0.2148	0.2300	0.0610
KHM-PHL	0.3566	0.2358	0.3481
KHM-SGP	0.1894	0.1894	0.0000
KHM-THA	0.2593	0.2537	0.0000
KHM-VNM	0.3492	0.1978	0.0119
LAO-MMR	0.1648	0.0700	0.5350
LAO-MYS	0.2329	0.1121	0.2689
LAO-PHL	0.1966	0.1058	0.5916
LAO-SGP	0.1502	0.0453	0.3300
LAO-THA	0.2118	0.1017	0.3300
LAO-VNM	0.3172	0.0509	0.3419
IDN-KHM	0.1748	0.1950	0.3096
IDN-LAO	0.2394	0.0887	0.2899
IDN-MMR	0.2427	0.1292	0.5230
IDN-MYS	0.2434	0.1607	0.3354
IDN-PHL	0.3384	0.1348	0.5478
IDN-SGP	0.1858	0.1014	0.3096
IDN-THA	0.2732	0.1651	0.3096

(continued)

Table A.8 (continued)

Country-Pair	SPS	TBT	INSP
IDN-VNM	0.2754	0.1060	0.3140
KHM-LAO	0.1928	0.1541	0.3300
KHM-MMR	0.2252	0.2200	0.2134
KHM-MYS	0.2148	0.2300	0.0610
KHM-PHL	0.3566	0.2358	0.3481
KHM-SGP	0.1894	0.1894	0.0000
KHM-THA	0.2593	0.2537	0.0000
KHM-VNM	0.3492	0.1978	0.0119
LAO-MMR	0.1648	0.0700	0.5350
LAO-MYS	0.2329	0.1121	0.2689
LAO-PHL	0.1966	0.1058	0.5916
LAO-SGP	0.1502	0.0453	0.3300
LAO-THA	0.2118	0.1017	0.3300
LAO-VNM	0.3172	0.0509	0.3419

Notes The RDs measured by construction is symmetric (see endnote 21). A higher value of RD (a value closer to one) indicates a higher regulatory dissimilarity between two countries. SPS—sanitary and phytosanitary measures; TBT—technical barriers to trade; INSP—pre-shipment inspection and other formalities
Source Calculated from UNCTAD-TRAINS (2021)

Notes

1. Trade in intermediates is direct evidence of the fragmentation of the production chain across borders (Johnson and Noguera 2012; Obashi and Kimura 2016).
2. Also called by various other names, such as fragmentation, production networks, production sharing or vertical specialization of production, refers to the phenomenon of slicing up the production into activities and tasks carried out in different countries.
3. Transmission mechanism here means the propagation of shocks in a foreign economy to domestic (endogenous) variables (output) through the international trade in merchandise goods.
4. The "bullwhip" is an effect where a final demand shock causes large changes in demand for intermediates, and firms adjust their inventories along the supply chain to new expected levels of demand.
5. We do not address directly other implications of intermediate goods trade, that is how trade elasticities and product substitution may amplify output shock transmission.
6. These countries are selected because of their high degree of integration of their manufacturing sectors in international production chains, and their reliance on imported inputs rather than domestic ones.
7. Capital goods are considered as intermediate goods and therefore included with the latter.
8. Production chains can be measured using three different methods: firm surveys to account for the fragmentation of the value chain; foreign trade statistics using parts and components/intermediate goods/value-added in trade flows

M. Raghavan et al., *China and ASEAN: Pivoting Trade and Shock Transmission*, https://doi.org/10.1007/978-981-16-1618-1

as an indicator for increased international production sharing; international input–output tables that relate the output of one industry to the inputs of other industries.

9. RCEP sub-group in this study refers to the non-ASEAN RCEP members (and excluding China, since the "China factor", the focal point of this study is examined separately), which are Japan, South Korea, India, Australia and New Zealand. Though India withdrew from the RCEP in November 2019, it is still considered in the sample as there are still efforts underway by RCEP to garner India's support. As an original negotiating party to the RCEP, India is given a special accession opportunity where the 18-month timeframe for accession is waived. All the five countries are considered extra-regional from the ASEAN perspective.
10. The FVA share indicates what part of a country's gross exports consists of inputs that have been produced in other countries.
11. Viet Nam, the Philippines, Brunei, and Malaysia have been locked in territorial disputes with China.
12. ASEAN calls it the ASEAN–China Free Trade Area (ACFTA), while China calls it the China–ASEAN Free Trade Area (CAFTA).
13. Some ASEAN countries, such as Singapore, took unilateral actions to improve their trade relations with China. Singapore concluded the China-Singapore Free Trade Agreement (CSFTA) in 2008.
14. Domestically produced inputs can also include some foreign inputs, and likewise, some foreign inputs can incorporate domestic value added exported in an earlier stage of the value chain.
15. It is acknowledged that trade in capital and intermediates only tell half the story of production chains.
16. Country A is said to have a RCA in a given product *i* when its ratio of exports of product *i* to its total exports of all goods (products) exceeds the same ratio for the world as a whole:

$$RCA_{Ai} = \frac{\frac{X_{Ai}}{\sum_{j\in p} X_{Aj}}}{\frac{X_{wi}}{\sum_{j\in p} X_{wj}}} \geq 1$$

where

- P is the set of all products (with $i \in P$),
- X_{Ai} is the country A's exports of product *i*,
- X_{wi} is the worlds's exports of product *i*,
- $\Sigma_{j\in P} X_{Aj}$ is the country A's total exports (of all products *j* in *P*), and
- $\Sigma_{j\in P} X_{wj}$ is the world's total exports (of all products *j* in *P*).

17. Comparative advantage does not mean competitiveness. This is because the calculation of the RCA based on gross exports instead of value-added exports may overestimate the export strength of countries, especially for countries that

have large export shares but not contain large shares of added value in their exports.

18. Concentration index, also named Herfindahl–Hirschman Index (Product HHI), is a measure of the degree of product concentration. An index value closer to 1 indicates a country's exports or imports are highly concentrated on a few products. On the contrary, values closer to 0 reflect exports or imports are more homogeneously distributed among a series of products. The following normalized HHI is used in order to obtain values between 0 and 1:

$$H_j = \frac{\sqrt{\sum_{i=1}^{n} \left(\frac{x_{ij}}{X_\infty}\right)^2} - \sqrt{1/n}}{1 - \sqrt{1/n}}$$

where
Hj = country or country group index.
xij = value of export for country *j* and product *i*
and

$$X_j = \sum_{i=1}^{n} x_{ij}$$

n = number of products (SITC Revision 3 at 3-digit group level).

19. The focus on the trade channel is justified as it is more relevant for ASEAN, relative to monetary and financial shocks.
20. However, one should note that output growth rate is not the only means of describing the business cycle as there could be a variety of other reasons (see Baxter and King 1995).
21. Identifying the sources of the shocks, that is, whether they are due to demand, supply or productivity is not the focus of our analysis.
22. Food security is a complex and multifaceted concept, comprising the criteria of availability (depends on domestic supplies, stocks and trade), access (influenced by income, employment and poverty), utilization (depends on food quality, health services, water and sanitation infrastructure, education, and female empowerment) and stability (requires consistent physical and economic access and proper utilization).
23. Since the NTM database of UNCTAD-TRAINS is based on the harmonized system (HS), the food sector refers to 18 products at the HS 2-digit level, HS2–HS4, HS7–HS13 and HS15–HS22 (see Table A.7 for the product description).
24. Technical measures comprise SPS, TBTs and pre-shipment inspection and other formalities (INSP).
25. The SPS includes measures to protect human, animal, or plant life or health.
26. The RD is calculated as follow. Let *i* (importer) and *j* (exporter) index countries, *k* products and *l* NTM types, and let:

$$NTM_{ilk} = \begin{cases} 1 \text{ if country } i \text{ imposes } l \text{ to product } k \\ 0 \text{ otherwise} \end{cases}$$

If both countries impose the same regulatory measure for product k at the HS6-digit, we code them as 0. In case if the regulatory measures differ between both the trading partners, we then code it as 1. This is measured for each measure-product pair for each country i and country j in bilateral sense. The RD is then calculated as $RD_{ik} = |NTM_{ilk} - NTM_{jlk}|$.
We then aggregated the RD over all measures and all products to HS 2-digit to obtain the overall dissimilarity measure. As such, the aggregate RD dissimilarity is the total sum of absolute values of the differences in NTM application between countries i and$j$ as follows:

$$RDs = \frac{1}{N}\sum_k\sum_l |NTM_{ilk} - NTM_{jlk}|$$

The RD values lie between 0 and 1, since it is normalized by the grand total of product-NTM pairs.

27. The end-year of the data is 2018, subject to the availability of the data at the time of the study, and therefore does not cover the US-China trade war and the global pandemic.

Index

M. Raghavan et al., *China and ASEAN: Pivoting Trade and Shock Transmission*,
https://doi.org/10.1007/978-981-16-1618-1